Inhuma

Inhuman States

Imprisonment, Detention and Torture in Europe Today

ANTONIO CASSESE

Polity Press

This English translation copyright © Polity Press 1996.
First published in Italy as *Umano–Disumano: Commissariati e prigioni
nell'Europa di oggi* copyright © Gius. Laterza & Figli, 1994.
This translation first published 1996 by Polity Press in association with
Blackwell Publishers Ltd.

Translated by Jennifer Greensleaves.

. 2 4 6 8 10 9 7 5 3 1

Editorial office:
Polity Press
65 Bridge Street
Cambridge CB2 1UR, UK

Marketing and production:
Blackwell Publishers Ltd
108 Cowley Road
Oxford OX4 1JF, UK

Published in the USA by:
Blackwell Publishers Inc.
238 Main Street
Cambridge, MA 02142, USA

ISBN 0–7456–1721–2
ISBN 0–7456–1722–0 (pbk)

A CIP catalogue record for this book is available from the British Library
and the Library of Congress.

Typeset in Plantin 11 on 12.5 pt
by CentraCet Ltd, Cambridge
Printed in Great Britain by T J Press Ltd, Padstow, Cornwall

This book is printed on acid-free paper.

Contents

I shall be happy if [. . .] I can obtain the secret thanks of the obscure and peaceful disciples of reason, and excite the tender emotion by which sensible minds sympathize with him who pleads the cause of humanity!

Cesare Beccaria, *Dei delitti e delle pene*, 1764, Introduction

Preface

From 1989 to 1993 I presided over a group of international inspectors whose job it was to visit police stations, prisons, barracks, psychiatric hospitals, detention centres for foreigners and any other places in which individuals had been deprived of their liberty by a state authority. This we did on behalf of twenty-three member states of the Council of Europe. The countries we were to visit belonged to 'Western' Europe (in the political, rather than geographical, sense, because they included Cyprus, in Asia, and Turkey, which straddles the two continents). Our specific mandate was to find out whether cruel, inhuman or degrading treatment, especially torture, had been inflicted on detainees. On a more general plane, we had to prevent conditions of detention that would violate the principles of humane behaviour.

Needless to say these states had granted us the right of inspection on condition we complied with certain restrictions. Above all our findings were to remain secret, our report on the state we had just inspected being transmitted in greatest secrecy to its government. In Strasbourg – the main seat of our activities – I remember thinking, as I was being sworn in, how shall I keep to myself all the pain and sadness of what I shall witness without that intense relief of being able to talk about it to those who are dearest to me. I was reminded of a story from my childhood about a girl who had been warned, on pain of death, never to tell a soul about what she saw and heard in the dingy inn where she worked; unable to bear the burden any longer, she describes what she has seen and heard to the cane-brake near the inn; then one day she discovers to her horror that, with every breath of wind, the rustling and shivering canes broadcast her whispered secrets.

I too felt a strong urge to tell the cane-brake about the strange and bitter things I had seen and heard in those four years. My whispering took the form of writing down my impressions and experiences. I have done so in my own way; I have no fear that the canes will repeat what the establishment wishes to keep hidden from the public eye – and this may well be to the good. However, to keep the promise I made in Strasbourg, I omitted the names of the countries and towns and the exact location of the places we visited – except when our report had been made public by the government concerned or, in exceptional cases, by ourselves.

I hope these pages will have some meaning for others: for me, writing them has made the intolerable tolerable. They deal with many things we usually try to ignore or to forget: violence, wickedness, aggressiveness, as well as contempt and indifference for our fellows. They wish to give tangible form to what is 'humane' as well as to what is 'inhuman'. They deal with places where contemporary society shuts away those people who are regarded as misfits or pariahs. We are perfectly aware that these places exist, but we would rather not know where – as with the land of the Cimmerians, a land of unknown location believed by the ancients to have been shrouded in darkness and fog. These are places where our 'negativity' is stacked away, as if it did not crop up continually around and even inside us – *inhumani nihil a me alienum puto*, to alter slightly the words of Terence.

In the following pages I shall also speak of Europe (by this I mean not only 'Western' Europe, but Central and Eastern Europe, since the countries in these areas have already granted or will soon grant Strasbourg the right of inspection). Spotlit from a very specific angle, they reveal what is still backward and barbarous in the practices of many European countries, in areas and institutions to which the principles of the Enlightenment have hardly penetrated, hence where archaic forms of behaviour survive. Do you really believe that a united Europe will only be made up of banks, offices, customs houses, supermarkets, lawyers and doctors? If a united Europe is really to be what we want it to be, we will have to smarten up the dirty, worn-out part of the social fabric, the part we have left shrouded in darkness. High standards of civilization must be brought to bear on the seamier side of society, too. For we must be guided by the moral imperative for which human rights have to be universal; supported, in this, by purely utilitarian reasons, too: since laws in Europe are so numerous and varied, sooner or later each one of us could be dragged into a police station abroad, interrogated and sent to prison.

1

A Revolutionary Step

Over the last few years I have often wondered why the member states of the Council of Europe (the international organization responsible for instituting our group of inspectors, and whose seat is in Strasbourg) should have adopted such a courageous, or imprudent, course as to charge a team of international experts with inspecting places that are usually out of bounds even to many national bodies, let alone to the ordinary citizen. Indeed, to set up such a body of inspectors (known officially as the European Committee for the Prevention of Torture and Inhuman or Degrading Treatment or Punishment) was to take a quite extraordinary step.

Never, in the history of international affairs, had a multinational group of persons – independent of government control – been granted formal authority to penetrate the *sancta sanctorum* of each state (police stations, prisons, psychiatric hospitals, etc.), in other words those very places where national sovereignty is given its overpowering yet most recondite expression. The very concept of 'national sovereignty' may seem purely legal and abstract to us. Yet one bears the brunt of this sovereignty whenever one is brought face to face with the rigours of law enforcement: whenever one is arrested and then questioned by a public prosecutor or police officers, whenever one is locked up in a cell or transferred to jail pending trial, whenever one is tried and then sentenced to prison. One also feels the weight of the full authority of the state whenever one demands the protection of law enforcement officials: whenever one asks the police to catch a criminal, or goes before a judge to demand justice. Laws are abstract and most people have only a scanty and remote knowledge of them. Yet the bewigged or uniformed men who translate those laws into the prescriptions that govern our daily doings, those men are, indeed, clearly visible to us. They are the state, they embody 'state sovereignty'. No wonder Hobbes warned us that without the sword the words of the law were empty vessels. However, it is precisely because those men and the state machinery they represent form the quintessence of national sovereignty, that modern states – still so reluctant to set aside their nationalist blinkers – consider this repressive machinery an inner sanctum to which no other state, let alone an international body, may gain access.

For the first time in history the (then) twenty-three member states of the Council of Europe have broken with this tradition. If we are to comprehend the full scope of this volte-face, we should place the creation of the Strasbourg group of inspectors in a broader historical perspective. Let us, then, step back into the eighteenth century, with Michel Foucault for our guide.

The French essayist and historian described, in *Discipline and Punish*, how, up to the first half of the eighteenth century in most European states (with the notable exception of Great Britain), all criminal trials were secret right up to the final sentence. Not only the public, but the accused, were kept in the dark as to what was going on in the courts: they did not know whether or not there was valid proof of the crime, they knew nothing of the judges' findings, of how they reached their decisions, or, indeed, of the reasons for their sentence. By contrast, punishment was in full view: meant to be a public spectacle. Read, for example, the well-known contemporary accounts of how those who had been declared guilty were hanged, beheaded or drawn and quartered. Towards the end of the eighteenth century this state of affairs was reversed. Corporal punishment gradually disappeared, while the form of punishment most commonly meted out was imprisonment. What is more, as the ideas of the Enlightenment spread, trials and the reasons for court decisions were made public. At the same time, capital punishment was hidden away, and the prisoner was executed far from the prying eyes of the public. The prisoner was secreted in remote institutions, prisons were supervised by 'bureaucrats' of punishment, prison guards, to whom society gave the job of acting as 'moral orthopaedists'. Thus, 'social dustbins' were set up which became the receptacles for the 'reprobates', banished from sight so that they might not pollute the 'healthy' members of society.

In recent times prisons have, fortunately, become less impenetrable to the outside world. The creation, by the Council of Europe, of an international body of inspectors is an important stage in the process leading to greater transparency. The states of Western Europe have decided to open their detention centres to international scrutiny. In other words, these places of detention can be inspected by experts who are not nationals of the country being visited, who can thus guarantee the maximum rigour, independence and impartiality in their remarks, and who will gradually establish a corpus of European standards and ensure their enforcement in both prisons and police stations. Thus, not only are trials, convictions and punishments made public, but the way in which punishment is meted out can now become part of the public domain, that is, subject to public scrutiny. Moreover, all proceedings and measures that precede a trial, such as police custody, are now open to international inspection.

Let me add that these European states have taken this important step at a time some might consider to be the least suitable for international transparency. As we all know, we are witnessing an exponential increase in crime. The buying and selling of drugs, throughout the world, with the support of frightening criminal organization, has had an unpredictable effect not only on the fabric of society, but specifically on prison life, whose internal organization has been disrupted, and is often dominated and conditioned, by the sale and the consumption of drugs. To this one should add terrorism, organized crime, and all those offences connected with such social ills as unemployment, immigration, ethnic and racial conflict. The structure of the modern state is today subject to enormous tension; governments are often hard put to find a social or political way out and they fall back increasingly on repressive measures. Yet, precisely when most countries have adopted repressive solutions, the member states of the Council of Europe have decided to subject to international scrutiny the violence that they employ – whether legally or illegally – against those who have been found guilty of crimes, or have been accused of committing a crime. In the name of the highest principles of democracy, transparency and civilization, these states have solemnly pledged to allow a supranational body to oversee how they treat the people they arrest and imprison. In other words, these European countries have accepted that inspectors will investigate whether each state has itself violated the rules of humane behaviour and respect for the individual that the criminals have, or may have, disregarded.

Why, then, have these states decided to cross the Rubicon? Why have states – those 'cold monsters', as Nietzsche called them, those gigantic, complicated

4

machines with no soul – decided, if not to flagellate themselves, at least to uncover their shameful parts and risk censure and perhaps opprobrium at the hands of an international body? There are various reasons for this.

The prime mover behind this decision was a Swiss banker, Jean-Jacques Gautier. For many years he had worked for the International Committee of the Red Cross, an organization with over a hundred years' experience of humanitarian aid, including visits to prisoner-of-war camps (besides, in times of peace and with the consent of the government concerned, visits to jails where political prisoners are detained). These experiences had made a profound impression on Gautier, a deeply religious man, and had induced him to set up a private association (the Swiss Committee against Torture) and, later, to suggest the creation of an international body, with broader powers than those of the International Committee of the Red Cross, that could inspect all places of detention, not only prisons and prisoner-of-war camps. During the last years of his life he lobbied intensely for this cause, with all the enthusiasm of a visionary. When, in 1980, his dream of creating a world body dealing with torture within the framework of the United Nations was shattered by the determined opposition of many Latin American, African, Asiatic and Eastern European countries, Gautier did not lose heart; he decided to approach the countries of Western Europe and found willing ears among individuals and governments in the Council of Europe. Thus, the prophetic vision and the tenacity of one man were the point of departure for that grand undertaking that was to bear fruit in 1987. Voltaire was indeed wrong when he quipped that, should one see a Swiss banker leaping out of a window, one should follow suit: there was certainly money to be made. There are some Swiss bankers who are not restricted by thoughts of amassing money, but are driven by lofty aspirations. Let us not forget that it was another Swiss businessman, Henri Dunant, who founded the International Red Cross more than a hundred years ago: in 1859, quite by chance, he had been passing through Solferino (a small town in northern Italy) and had been horrified by the massacre in the battle between the united forces of France and Piedmont, on the one hand, and of Austria on the other. I feel it is significant that the oldest and youngest of humanitarian organizations, the International Red Cross and the Council of Europe's Committee, should both be the offspring of the generous concern of Swiss men.

However, the vision and enthusiasm of one man are not sufficient to construct a complex international mechanism, especially when it has been designed to cramp the exclusive authority of sovereign states, at least in one specific sector. In reality, much is due to the open attitude of numerous governments of Western Europe, an attitude that has been influenced by the ideology of human rights. The force of that ideology, as it spread throughout the world after 1948 when the Universal Declaration was adopted by the UN General Assembly, has been immense. Day after day, the principles of that Declaration – fleshed out in Europe by the 1950 Convention on Human Rights – have been instilled in the minds of rulers and peoples, not only thanks to the work of the United Nations and the Council of Europe, but also to that of such non-governmental organizations as Amnesty International. The Italian philosopher Tommaso Campanella was quite right when he claimed that durable human movements are set in motion first by words and then by the sword. It is beyond doubt that not a few contemporary statesmen, especially in the field of international affairs (such as foreign ministers), are more and more disposed to listen to those who insist on respect for human rights. Such men, mindful of *Realpolitik*, often try to win over their more reluctant colleagues (such as the ministers of defence and justice). Furthermore, they may, on occasion, play an active role in shaking state bureaucracies out of their torpor and recalcitrance, this being the main obstacle to any 'meddling' from the international community.

However, there is perhaps a third motive. Quite a few Western states do not possess their own system of inspection for prisons and other places of detention. That is they are unable, at a national level, to carry out a minute and effective scrutiny of how the state machinery works in such shadowy areas as police stations, prisons, psychiatric institutions, barracks, and so on. Police officers, warders and the military do not like to be supervised. There are bureaucratic barriers to inspection; the force of tradition is a hindrance, but so is public opinion – since there is a general clamour in our countries to ensure that 'criminals' receive the severest punishment, but little interest in possible abuse to which they can be subjected. This may be why these countries have eventually realized that it is easier to delegate the monitoring of places of detention to an international body. It became apparent that to set up such a body, using diplomatic channels for this purpose, would be one way to circumvent and defeat national resistance to such inspection.

Yet another motive is worth mentioning: the upper echelons of state bureaucracy – diplomats, politicians, civil servants and men of law – who had a hand in the drafting of the international treaty by which the Committee was set up, may not have understood its implications once it came into effect – these implications became apparent only gradually. It was certainly difficult to foresee the multifarious impact the labours of the inspectors would have on the inner workings of the various states. Nevertheless, and by some happy chance, these foreign ministry engineers acted with insouciance; many of them might have balked at taking such a daring step had they anticipated the explosive force of the mechanism they were about to set in motion.

Let me make one last remark. Although the group of inspectors came into being in Western Europe, this does not mean that this is an area which more than any other needs international supervision to prevent inhuman or degrading treatment, and torture in particular. Unfortunately, it is the other areas of the globe – especially Latin America, Africa and certain Asian countries – that need such inspection most. If this body has been set up by Western European countries, this is due, as I have already remarked, to the fact that these states are more aware of the need for international monitoring. Let us hope that, little by little, this experience will cross frontiers and oceans and spread to the other areas of the world.

2

The Blue Berets of
Human Rights?

When the French National Assembly was discussing the
international convention by which the Strasbourg Committee was set up, the Foreign Minister, Roland Dumas,
speaking enthusiastically in favour of its ratification,
described the inspectors as 'blue berets of human rights'.
The definition is graphic, but imprecise. Let us take a look
at what the real powers of the inspectors are, and how they
are wielded.

During the drafting of the Convention, when we began
to discuss the procedures the future Committee should
follow, some suggested inspections should be unexpected:
states should not be forewarned either of the dates or of
the places to be inspected. Others counselled a more
prudent line: a sovereign state cannot be treated like a
thief who must be caught red-handed. Since the Committee owed its existence to a decision taken by these very
states, the inspectors had to show consideration for the
'sensibilities' of their sires, as well as for the forms and
rituals to which they are so attached. The drafters thus
divided into two groups: the 'strict disciplinarians', and
the 'moderates' who wanted to respect the dignity of
governments. Since we had reached a deadlock, we asked
advice of the International Committee of the Red Cross,

the only international body with vast experience of supervision in the humanitarian field.

They came and gave us the following warning: 'Do not suppose you can descend upon a state and take it by surprise. Even if you did not announce your visit, it has its own channels of information and will be alerted as soon as you cross the frontier, or arrive in one of its airports. Besides, you will not be able to begin your inspection until you have contacted the relevant ministry and received information on the whereabouts of all the places of detention, the number and categories of inmates, and so on. Do not imagine you can make a surprise visit to a prison. Jails are complex organizations with a rigid hierarchical structure. If you do not warn them of your impending arrival, and the governor does not give orders for your reception, you will be left waiting out in the cold for many hours. For the same reason, the complex machinery of prisons will make it difficult for them to transfer elsewhere the dozens of prisoners they may not want you to see, or even to transform in a couple of days the conditions of detention (capacity and overcrowding in the cells, sanitary arrangements, prison work and other activities, sports and recreation facilities, procedures for visits from the prisoners' families, etc.). The same goes for psychiatric hospitals and similar institutions. As for police stations, do not fancy you can take them by surprise; the few minutes it takes to have a cup of coffee with the superintendent will be enough to whisk out of the building any detainee he might not want you to see, or to remove "unpresentable" objects. Hence – except in very special circumstances – the key to effective inspections is not so much surprise as meticulous attention to detail, tenacity, flair and experience.'

This advice was utterly convincing. We decided to opt for a mixed procedure: we would warn the government concerned a few weeks in advance of the dates of our arrival and the composition of our delegation, and a couple of days before arriving we would indicate which institutions we intended to visit, with the proviso that once we were in the country we might suddenly choose to inspect other institutions, or (in the case of jails or psychiatric hospitals) give an hour's warning, so the director had time to organize our reception.

We also decided that, if our visits were to be effective, the inspectors should be granted unlimited power to visit all places of detention, as well as the right to speak in private (that is, out of the hearing of any authority) to both the detainees and to any others we saw fit to 'interrogate' (police and prison officers, doctors, private organizations for the protection of human rights, the officials of the relevant trade unions, the prisoners' relatives, etc.). We also reserved the right to collect any information or documentation we thought necessary to our inquiry.

At this point some delegates from the governments concerned objected that certain state prerogatives had to be respected. For example, they stated, take the case of an inspection to high-security cells for the military; if these are in a secret military base, or in a base containing secret plants – nuclear ones for example – that are not accessible to civilians, the inspectors' visit might occasion dangerous leaks. The same argument was valid, they observed, whenever the inspectors wished to speak to terrorists held in high-security jails; if the authorities had decided to keep the place of their detention secret, the inspectors' interview might, even involuntarily, lead to vital information being disclosed and, unwittingly, passed on to members of the terrorist group still at large. Another objection was that the inspectors might want to speak to people in police custody, who were being questioned by police officers or by the inquiring magistrate: here the international inspector's 'intrusion' might harm the judicial inquiry, or offend against the rules of that country's criminal procedure.

Naturally, we had to take all these criticisms into account. In the end we managed to find solutions that preserved the right of the inspectors to carry out their investigations without damaging certain vital interests of the state, so long as there was some justification for doing so. Thus, it was agreed that, should the inspectors visit a military base, they would scrutinize only its detention centres, and not move freely about the base itself; alternatively, the government would transfer military prisoners to be interviewed to a place that was not secret. The solution for terrorists was to question them without asking for their names and date of birth, or looking at their files. As for people presently being questioned pending trial, it was agreed that we might decide to postpone our interview to a later date. In a nutshell, for each case a formula was found which respected both the humanitarian intent of the inspection and the requirements of the state, and was such as not to limit the scope of the inspectors' investigation.

We all agreed on the need to select inspectors on account of their competence, experience and rigour. Consequently, it was decided that, unlike other international monitoring agencies (usually composed of men of law and diplomats), our Committee was to include – besides experts in human rights or criminal law – doctors, psychiatrists, psychologists, experts in forensic medicine or penitentiaries. We also decided that each delegation of inspectors could, on occasion, appoint experts, on a case by case basis, to supplement the competence of the group, according to the requirements of each visit.

Finally, it was decided to differentiate between two types of inspection: ordinary or routine ones, and *ad hoc* inspections. The former would be carried out periodically in each of the twenty-three countries, to investigate, little by little, all places of detention. *Ad hoc* visits occur in answer to the call of particularly serious and urgent cases: when the Committee receives persistent, alarming and reliable information of flagrant violations in certain detention centres of a given country, it can decide to send a delegation to inspect only the relevant institutions. These are 'targeted' visits, made for a specific purpose, and are not based on general or objective criteria (such as choosing the state to be visited by drawing lots, as is the case with the periodic visits) but on the 'policy' choice of the Committee. However, the procedures adopted are no different for the *ad hoc* visits: here, too, forewarning is given to the country in question.

A crucial issue was to decide what sanctions could be applied by the inspectors. On this point the states were adamant. Having granted broad powers of inspection to the Committee, this largesse had to be counterbalanced by preventing the inspectors from making the deviant behaviour of authorities public, let alone allowing them to impose coercive sanctions on the erring state. In the end it was agreed the inspectors would hand their report, with its conclusions and recommendations, in strict confidence to the proper authorities of that state. Though enforcement proper was excluded, it was decided that, in exceptional cases, when a state refused to cooperate or to implement the inspectors' recommendations, the Committee could apply a moral 'sanction' – agreed to by two thirds of Committee members – by informing public opinion of the state's non-fulfilment of its duties.

The Committee's frame of reference should now be clear. The Strasbourg inspectors are the very reverse of Amnesty International, at least from certain points of view. Amnesty is a non-governmental organization which operates throughout the world, defends the rights of single prisoners, and can base its work on information obtained from both the victims (and from their relatives or other human rights associations), or from government authorities, or by sending observers to public trials. It has no right of inspection and, thus, cannot determine possible cases of abuse or violation at first hand. However, it can make its findings public: denouncing violations and appealing to public opinion are its most effective weapons. The Strasbourg Committee, by contrast, was set up by European governments and its sphere is limited to Europe; whereas it has broad powers of inspection, it does not defend the rights of single prisoners, but scrutinizes their conditions of detention and aims to prevent abuses. It can collect documentary proof and question witnesses and the alleged victims of abuse. Above all, it can inspect places of detention without being hampered by the authorities. There is, however, a heavy price to pay for such freedom of action: the inspectors' work is subject to the hatchet of secrecy. Their report must be confidential, and only in exceptional cases (such as those mentioned above) can they appeal to public opinion.

In many ways the Committee's powers are similar to those of the International Committee of the Red Cross. It, too, has wide powers of inspection in detention camps (whether under the Geneva Conventions, or on the strength of specific agreements with the interested states). It, too, must operate in the greatest secrecy, without informing public opinion of the results of its visits. On other points the two committees are different. The Strasbourg Committee's inspections are intended to prevent inhuman or degrading situations and it cannot protect individual detainees; furthermore, it can visit other places of detention such as police stations, in addition to state prisons. The International Committee of the Red Cross is there to protect the individual (with humanitarian aid, including food parcels and medicine), and may regularly visit only 'political prisoners' or other detainees 'at risk' (because of armed conflict or civil disorder) in penitentiaries or internment camps.

The Blue Berets of Human Rights?

In the following chapters I hope to show how the balance between secrecy (stemming from cooperation with the specific government) and publicity (the upshot of a government's failure to cooperate) has made the Strasbourg Committee's work fruitful and effective.

3

Firemen or Specialists in Preventive Medicine?

So far, I have described the powers of the Strasbourg inspectors. But what is their specific mission? Hardly that of being firemen: they are not called in to put out fires. On occasion there may be a need for urgent inspection after serious, reliable and consistent reports have been received of cruelty or large-scale abuse in a given country (these provoke the so-called *ad hoc* visits I mentioned in the previous chapter). It is primarily in such cases that the inspectors should discover serious cases of ill-treatment and induce the erring state to put an end to them immediately. Of course, during their periodic visits, the inspectors must also be on the alert for cases of violence and oppression against individuals deprived of their liberty. Yet their main task is prevention.

The governments were wise, in drafting the Convention, when they decided that for one thing the Committee monitoring conditions of detention should not be a judicial body (since the latter would only intervene in answer to specific complaints alleging that the rights of an individual had been violated); for another, that the Committee should not confine itself to fact-finding. It was agreed that, as far as many rights were concerned, it was vital to intervene *before* violations had been made. Indeed, prevention is becoming more and more important in the field of human rights. For example, what is the sense of intervening after a person's right to secret correspondence has been violated and details of his or her private life have been made public? Is it enough to condemn the guilty official and possibly to pay compensation? Likewise, if during a judicial inquiry the rule of secrecy has been disregarded, what financial compensation can there be for the irreparable damage done to the accused's reputation? When a person has been apprehended by the police or imprisoned illegally, can subsequent release and damages paid by the state ever make good such a grave breach of a fundamental right? Above all, when a person has been physically maltreated or subjected to psychological violence, or worse to torture, how can the sentencing of the culprits or possible compensation ever erase the scars from the victim's mind and body? In most cases to intervene *after* a violation is relatively useless.

Let me add a fact which was borne in on me during my four years' work among detainees: many violations of human rights are never remedied at all, not even at the judicial level, for the simple reason that the victims do not rebel: they make no official protest. I was very perturbed by this and asked many of the detainees I interviewed why they had not denounced the abuses or claimed compensation. Many were unable to answer. I believe their inertia, when faced with abuse and violence, has various causes.

These include subjective factors, such as a poor education or scant moral awareness (we do well to remember that ninety per cent of those who suffer abuse come from the underprivileged classes and are ignorant of their rights). There is an element of fatalism, too. An uneasy conscience can be a contributory factor; if, by committing a crime or any other offence, you feel you are in the wrong, you may think you have no right to protest against ill-treatment by law enforcement officers. In some cases the inmate knows, from previous experience, how futile it is to raise one's voice against abuse, or claim compensation. Sometimes, the victim may fear renewed violence. Let me mention an exemplary case quoted by one who witnessed an instance of serious ill-treatment. The man had been imprisoned for political crimes, years earlier. One night he heard desperate cries coming from the section for common criminals. The next day, as he happened to be talking to the supervisory judge (a man in the old mould, true to his principles despite the oppressive political climate prevailing in the country at that time), he asked him to check whether anyone had been tortured the previous night in that section. The very same evening the judge summoned him and warned him severely to say nothing and forget what had happened. He explained that he had soon discovered an inmate who had been brutally beaten up. When asked who had done this to him, the man said he had been bruised falling downstairs. The motive for this improbable answer was obvious, the judge felt; in that prison it was possible to earn a little money, and on the whole conditions were not bad; the warders who had beaten the man – a notorious rebel – had threatened to transfer him to a worse prison if he talked.

Objective factors are also important. First, it is often difficult to present proof of abuses: as we shall see in chapter 6, modern forms of torture either leave no trace on the body, or the traces disappear soon after; besides, it is difficult to produce witnesses, since ill-treatment is usually carried out in the privacy of a cell or in the office of a police station. Nor should we forget that many state systems are legally well equipped to repress both deviant behaviour and possible protests against police violence. For instance, police officers can bring a charge of slander against anyone they have arrested and are holding in custody, if the latter accuses them of brutality; as has happened more than once, prison officers can accuse

18

detainees of 'contempt of a public official'; as a result, the prisoner in question (even one under a short sentence) may lose many privileges, such as the right to prison leave or to penalties alternative to detention.

It is all these reasons that make *prevention* so crucial, especially for those who have been deprived of their liberty. Hence, the governments did well, in 1987, to set up a body of inspectors who intervene – not like firemen or doctors called to a patient's deathbed – but as specialists in preventive medicine, whose job is to recognize the sources and agents of epidemics and to take all the steps that will eliminate the dangerous hotbeds of infection.

You may well ask, what form does prevention take when it concerns people deprived of their liberty? What steps can the inspectors adopt to fulfil their mission?

Since it was our remit to prevent abuses and ill-treatment, we had to take note of any situation, however acceptable *per se*, that might lead to the inhuman or degrading treatment of inmates if combined with other factors. We also examined any situation belonging to that no-man's-land that made them neither entirely acceptable nor subject to censure. These belong to an intermediate area lying between what is 'humane' and what is 'contrary to the principles of humanity'; a high-risk area, because behaviour and circumstances can degenerate and become intolerable. As a result of interpreting our mandate in these terms, the field of our investigations became immense. Let me give an example.

Take police stations. Obviously, when we carry out our inspections, we start by asking the people held there if they have been ill-treated, beaten up, or otherwise harassed. But that is not all. We examine police cells to see if they are salubrious and adequate in size; we measure them one by one, check ventilation and natural and artificial sources of light, hygiene (we have frequently found vermin or traces of blood and excrement) and toilet facilities; we also inquire whether showers and washing facilities are available, whether people held in custody get a hot meal, whether it is possible to call the policeman standing guard in emergencies (whether there is a bell in the cell, or whether, as in many countries, inmates have to beat insistently on the door to attract the guard's attention). We also scrutinize the custody record, to establish the flux of detainees, the average period of detention and whether there is any record of family visits or meetings with a lawyer or with the medical officer.

Why do we investigate so many things? Our aim is to verify whether conditions of detention in police stations are so poor as to be inhuman and degrading. However, even when the threshold to situations at risk is not overstepped, these conditions can signal a degenerative process. For example, if detainees are kept for hours or days on end in dirty and unhealthy premises, with little food, in dreary and unhealthy inactivity, they are far more vulnerable to police pressure (as well as being confirmed in their criminal bent). Guilty or innocent, those people are forced – for no good reason – to spend hours and days in dingy squalor. If nothing is done, the situation can deteriorate. Similarly, the police can get so used to the situation that they will end up regarding the detainees not as human beings, but as things.

Our inquiries do not stop here. We also ascertain whether, in the days preceding our visit, many people have been released (or transferred to prison), or if there is anything abnormal in the absence of detainees at the time of our inspection. We scrutinize the offices where the police hold their interrogations, check the weapons and other coercive instruments they possess (for instance, whether they use regulation truncheons, or if they possess prohibited weapons or instruments, if they have electric batons, and so on).

Besides, we talk at length to police officers, not only to ascertain their level and kind of education, but also to inquire into precise points. In particular, whether the detainees enjoy, in practice as well as in theory, those four rights we consider fundamental: the right of access to a lawyer, the right to be seen by a doctor, the right to have their families notified of their detention, and that of being promptly informed of their basic rights. In our opinion, whether these rules are embodied in the legislation of the country and applied in practice is one of the decisive factors for ascertaining if people detained by the police are 'at risk'. When a person has been arrested and can count on those four rights, then there is an objective chance that the police will find it difficult to inflict inhuman or degrading treatment on him or her. On the other hand, if these rights, or some of them, are not enshrined in legislation or are not applied in practice, we know we have entered a 'danger zone': the objective defences are lacking that make ill-treatment less likely.

Given their importance, we do more than merely verify the existence of such guarantees: it is indeed all too easy to elude them. We try to establish in detail what goes on in actual practice. For instance, in one of the countries we visited, these guarantees exist and are normally applied. But various people detained for common crimes told us – in terms we found absolutely credible – that before and after being interrogated by the police in the presence of a lawyer, they had been subjected to pressure and intimidation and had even been beaten up. Later, the lawyer could do nothing for lack of proof, and also because the police officers threatened to accuse the detainee of slander, had there been a formal protest. In some other countries, police officers bypass the same rules by summoning the people suspected of crimes as 'witnesses': thus, they can be interrogated without the intrusive presence of a lawyer. At times, in countries where it is mandatory to carry a

21

personal ID card, the police arrest people and take them to the police station, either because they were without the necessary document, or to check its authenticity; slowly, while the necessary verification is being carried out, casual questions are made and a real interrogation is held, though of an informal and good-natured kind. Of course, the detainee could refuse to talk without a lawyer; but the police know that people are often uninformed of their rights and take them unawares. In many other states there is another, very widespread way to circumvent these rules. The device is contained in the rules themselves, which in exceptional cases allow the police to postpone the presence of the defence lawyer for many days. All that need be done is to claim exceptional circumstances, with the public prosecutor's approval, and question the suspect (although statements obtained in this manner cannot be used in evidence, precisely because they were given without the lawyer being present). Furthermore, in some countries police may use yet another legal expedient: as the relevant provision of the code of criminal procedure states that the 'accused' has a right to have a lawyer present, the police say that until a formal charge has been made, the detainee has no right to call a lawyer; they can then question the accused for hours or even for a whole day, without giving information on the nature of the purported crime until later, and only then granting the right to consult a lawyer.

It is easy to see that good laws and practice are not enough. A strong professional ethic must be inculcated into police officers; they must be well trained and taught to respect their fellow human beings. Besides, their professional training should include acceptable methods for obtaining information and confessions, and – when these are not forthcoming – investigation techniques other than those of interrogation.

Another aspect we always inquire about in countries

where it is not obligatory to have a defence lawyer present, is whether the suspect in police custody is hooded or blindfolded, before or during the interrogation; the practice is far more widespread than one might believe, and is a clear signal of possible ill-treatment. In some cases the police, while not admitting to having used such methods, claim there is some justification for them – especially with terrorists – so as to protect the police officer from recognition and, hence, from future attempts on his or her life. I remember a high-ranking judge admitting, candidly, that in his country policemen always blindfolded dangerous suspects and terrorists, before and during interrogation. He felt this was entirely justified: not only were the police protected, but the arrested person would not be able to draw a plan of the police station for future attacks on the building. He also thought it right, in the interests of the police, not to record the interrogating officers' names. Naturally, it is easy to rejoin that correct forms of interrogation are less likely to provoke reprisals. Furthermore, there are other ways of preventing recognition: in many countries the accused is questioned facing floodlights, with the policeman sitting at a desk out of sight (this technique, however, though less objectionable than blindfolding the prisoner, is still open to criticism, since it can be used to intimidate and bewilder).

Another important point we have to check is whether the national authorities keep a watch on detention (via administrative inspectors, representatives from the public prosecutor's office or the inquiring magistrate): the absence of such mechanisms increases the risks of abuse.

Despite what I have said so far, it has not always been easy to classify the situations we came across as likely to degenerate or belonging to those grey areas at risk. Quite the contrary! Let me quote one example I feel is significant.

In one of the northern countries we visited, Finland,

alcoholism is notoriously one of the great social ills. Especially during the weekends, the streets are often littered with drunks slumped on the pavements and apparently asleep, but usually almost comatose. The police gather them up and take them to the central police station, to cells specially set aside for this purpose in the Police Detoxification Centre. It is an act of charity; these people, who have committed no crime, are taken off the streets and prevented from freezing to death outside. However, if you go into this area in the Helsinki central police station, you will find the saddest of spectacles. A central room with sixteen small television screens allows you to look in on forty-five cells, some for only one inmate, others – by far the most numerous – for four or six. On the floor of each cell, white lines determine the exact space destined for a drunk. Each space is occupied by a body frozen in sleep: a sort of human parking lot. On average the 'parking lot' contains a hundred persons, but once, and for a whole day, it contained three hundred and twenty. Drunks are allowed to stay on the premises for no more than twelve hours (roughly the time required to come to one's senses and be able to move off). We were very perturbed by the sight and asked why beds or mattresses were not provided; the police explained that this could be dangerous: the drunks might fall off the bed and hurt themselves, and they had often been known to set fire unwittingly to the mattresses when lighting a cigarette.

That cell was a disturbing sight, partly because it was terrible to see people so dejected and humiliated as to fall into this subhuman state. However, could we consider this 'inhuman and degrading treatment'? With heavy hearts we decided this was not possible, the other alternative being for the police to leave the drunks on the streets. Yet, nevertheless, we felt we had to censure the Finnish authorities. First they could have provided low mattresses of noninflammable, easy-to-wash material. Then, we criticized the excessive levels of occupancy and, more specifically, the insufficient medical monitoring. A person can fall into a coma as a result of an acute form of diabetes, or for other medical reasons (such as internal haemorrhaging). We asked the authorities always to ascertain why these people lay senseless on the streets. We also asked them to keep the drunks 'parked' in their 'garage' under continual medical supervision, partly because after an initial phase of complete torpor they might become violent or aggressive, and also because they might have received traumas before being picked up. We felt that the absence of all these guarantees might lead to situations capable of degenerating or becoming inhuman, or even put the lives of these people in danger.

The aim of preventing ill-treatment means that our inquiries are even more complex whenever we inspect prisons and other penitentiary establishments. These are in fact social microcosms, with complicated and stratified structures, as well as their own codes and systems of punishment. Our job is to verify a vast number of factors: the size and capacity of cells, to determine possible cases of overcrowding; the state of sanitation; the quality and quantity of food; whether there are laboratories and workshops for vocational training, gymnasiums and other recreational opportunities, and courtyards for taking exercise; to what extent the medical service is qualified and thorough; interpersonal relations between warders and inmates; structures set aside for family and lawyers' visits; whether there are social workers and psychologists; opportunities for prisoners' complaints against abuse; the nature of punishment applied (especially forms of disciplinary confinement); whether there are forms of government supervision (such as administrative inspection or monitoring by supervisory judges). Once all these data have been collected, we have a fairly accurate picture of the prevailing climate in a prison, and can determine if there are

25

inhuman or degrading conditions or risk situations that could degenerate.

You could ask: having checked on ill-treatment at the hands of state authorities, do you also investigate and prevent violence between inmates? Naturally, we were well aware that there are high levels of hidden violence in penitentiaries among prisoners and that distinctions of class and hierarchy exist: some give orders, others execute them and others are the natural victims. But these are intangible phenomena for those who do not live in a prison for any length of time, and it is therefore difficult to grasp the logic of such behaviour or the channels through which it is expressed. Thus, usually we have not been able to discern cases of abuse of one inmate against another. In one case, however, the phenomenon had emerged into the open and become institutionalized. In the central prison in the capital of one of the Scandinavian countries, our inspectors received numerous and concurrent details of acts of violence committed by some prisoners against others. The category most at risk was that of drug addicts who had got into debt: if they did not pay up they were kicked, beaten up or knifed (though the weapon was often muffled, in part, by anything that came to hand so that the wounds would not be fatal). The atmosphere of terror was so widespread that many detainees had asked to be locked up in isolation, to ward off any further violence. The prison administration, even when it knew about this ill-treatment, did nothing. Our inspectors reached some highly critical conclusions about the prison authorities and demanded they draw up an effective plan for putting an end to the reign of terror in the jail. Even though the violence had not been perpetrated by the authorities themselves, their inertia was very much to blame: only they were able to take the necessary measures, hence they should have done something.

One delicate issue, which we have pondered more than

once in assessing the conditions of detention in the various countries, is whether the same parameters applied throughout, or whether we should take into account the economic and social conditions, as well as the historical background of each country. The Committee was divided on this point. Our medical colleagues felt ours should be a kind of 'scientific diagnosis', containing only an accurate description of what we had seen, and suggesting possible remedies; in other words, our task was to 'photograph' the situation and prescribe the 'necessary medicine'. Other members felt that the institutions we visited should be set in the context of each specific country, taken as a whole. How could we expect Spanish, Cypriot or Maltese prisons to satisfy the same standards as Swedish or Finnish jails? How could we ignore the specific history and degree of economic development of each state? How could we pretend that Swiss or Danish policemen and prison officers resemble their counterparts in, say, Italy or Greece?

After a lively debate and due reflection, we decided on the latter course, though with important modifications. We determined that the parameters for what is 'human' or 'inhuman' and 'degrading' should always be the same. We could not accept the idea of Europe as a Neapolitan ice-cream of cultural levels and degrees of development; 'mankind' and 'human' are universal concepts. Yet in applying the same set of canons we must not neglect the national conditions and history of each country. It certainly was not our intention to forgive shortcomings in view of the prevailing mentality, or the socio-economic development of a given state, but to pursue two goals. First, to gain a balanced view of specific conditions, their impact on the prevailing mentality in that country and, therefore, the extent to which they would be seen as inhuman or degrading by the parties involved. For instance, a noisy and crowded dormitory in prisons in a country such as Spain or Turkey would be experienced in other states (such as Norway or Finland) as an unbearable invasion of the inmates' privacy. By contrast, in Southern Europe such conditions are seen as a form of social relationship that are both acceptable and to be encouraged; detainees in these countries would find separate cells, with little chance to socialize, inhuman. I was once told by an ambassador from a French-speaking African country that when his fellow citizens were locked up in separate cells in European jails – by this he did not mean solitary confinement, of which I shall speak in chapter 4 – to them the experience was a form of torture. Second, if national factors are borne in mind, it is easier to work out adequate and realistic recommendations.

With these two exceptions, we have always agreed that our aim was to achieve the same level of civilized standards in the field of detention, throughout Europe.

4

Into the Breach:
Inspectors in Action

Four years of hard and passionate work bore fruit. In those years we were called on to make only three *ad hoc* visits (two to Turkey and one to Northern Ireland). Among ourselves we had come to call these 'Oh my God visits'. It is an expression we learnt from an English prison governor. After visiting his jail from top to bottom, we settled down to discuss our findings with him. In telling us about the various national inspections he had received in his career, he said he had learnt to recognize an imminent visit whenever his deputy picked up the phone and exclaimed, after a momentary pause, 'Oh my God!'

Of course, it has not been easy, especially in our first visit to each country, to get the authorities to accept that an international group of inspectors should enjoy such wide-ranging powers. These problems were greatest, not so much in prisons or big institutions – where the directors were used to being checked by their superiors – as in police stations. These are hardly ever subject to national inspection; even in countries where the judiciary has the power to verify what goes on there, it is almost unknown for a magistrate to set foot in a police station. Furthermore, the police are so used to investigating and interrogating people suspected of crimes that they find it inconceivable to be themselves the object of investigation, especially by foreigners. Besides, many modern states are notoriously slow, cumbersome and inefficient. In our case, this often meant that the central authorities had not informed the local ones of our arrival, nor had they explained what our job was or how extended our powers were. More than once this meant that we had animated altercations and had to display all our moral authority to be allowed in to see over the police station and to talk to the inmates without hindrance.

Some hostile encounters with state authorities

To give some idea of these wrangles and of our reactions, let me recount an incident that took place during one of our first visits. We were in a very large country. One evening we decided to inspect the police headquarters in the ministry. At half past nine a group from our delegation presented itself to the policeman on guard and asked to speak to the police inspector on duty that evening and to begin our visit. After various telephone calls, the man said he was sorry, the chief inspector was out of town and his deputy did not feel he had the authority to let us in. I pointed out that our Committee had informed the Ministry of the Interior a few days earlier that we intended to visit that police station, and showed him not only our international ID cards, but also a special document describing our powers in the language of that country. It made no difference. The policeman insisted it would be better to come back the next morning. One of our powers was to start an inspection any time we chose; I therefore told the policeman we would not move until we had been granted free access to the building. We settled down in a small room next to the guard room, whence I was able to phone officials in the various ministries, to protest and ask for immediate assistance to get on with our work. The tug of war went on until three thirty the next morning, when we were told the chief inspector was about to arrive. He turned up a little later, tall and fat and immaculately dressed, with a black moustache standing out against his freshly shaven face. He greeted us with a certain arrogance but was not able to conceal his embarrassment. After giving us the list of people held in custody, he proceeded to lecture us with a professorial air on the workings of the police in his country. After a little I cut him short and pointed out that we were interested in seeing the detention cells and wanted to begin our visit at once. He looked surprised: were we not feeling rather tired? Indeed, we were feeling weak with suppressed irritation at the obstacles placed in our way, and very tired after spending the previous day going round a prison. Nevertheless, we started off on our visit.

All the cells were empty except one, where we found an inmate looking bewildered and sickly, with a four-day stubble. As soon as he saw us he came forward with outstretched hand, saying emphatically: 'Welcome to this country. The police here behave extremely well!' We realized it was no use going on. After about an hour (it was five o'clock by now), we left the police station and went back to our hotel. We slept a few hours and then drafted an official protest to the Foreign Minister. We warned him in very polite terms that if another such incident were to occur, we would have to leave the country at once. The protest was sent off and we returned to the same prison we had visited the day before; that evening, at the same time as on our previous visit, we returned to the police headquarters. We were given immediate entry and were able to carry out our visit undisturbed, even though all the cells were empty – an unusual occurrence, if the custody record, which we examined with great care, were to be believed.

There was another incident, once again in a large police station, this time in the section for political detainees. Various prisoners – accused or convicted of terrorism – with whom we had spoken in two prisons in the same town, had given us detailed descriptions of the rooms in that police station in which they had been interrogated and brutalized. We had already visited that police station, and things did not tally. We had seen some of the cells described by the prisoners and not others. Since the descriptions were credible, we asked for further details and a plan of the building. One point, on which they all agreed, was that in going, blindfold, from the section we had seen to the one we had not recognized, they had all been forced to duck at a given point; we inferred that this must be a very low door. A couple of them said that, as the blindfold had slipped while they were bending down to enter the 'secret' area, they remembered seeing what looked like metal buckets full of sand, and other paraphernalia for putting out fires. Others had added that, on entering that area they had noticed a change: the air was drier and stagnant, certainly there was no humidity, nor ventilation, such as they had noticed elsewhere; besides, they had often heard the loud noise of vehicles coming in and going out nearby, which became inaudible once they had ducked under the low entrance. We concluded that the open area must be close to a garage, while the hidden one must be completely isolated, except for the low door.

Back in our hotel, we held a powwow. Ours was a sacrosanct right to visit all the places of detention of institutions under our jurisdiction; if what the prisoners had told us was true, the authorities had committed a grave breach of their obligations. We put our heads together, fitted the various pieces of information into a complete jigsaw and combined the different plans we had been given.

On the strength of this work, the next morning we went

early to the police station. They were surprised to see us again, as we had visited them twice already, each time with great thoroughness. We went round all the rooms on all the floors and, after a couple of hours, we came to a large room on the ground floor, close to a yard with a couple of cars; there we stopped to exchange impressions. We had noticed, near that sort of garage, a narrow corridor leading to a stair: in front of the first step, there was a neat row of rudimentary fire-extinguishing contraptions, including four metal buckets full of sand. If the 'hidden' area existed, it must be behind that wall; there had to be a small, concealed door there. After a rapid consultation among ourselves, we decided to cut the Gordian knot. I called back the police inspector who had come with us on our tour, and told him we presumed there was a door hidden in the wall: we asked him to open it and show us what it concealed. The poor man, who until then had been very helpful and ostentatiously well-mannered, turned white. He muttered that I must be mistaken: it was just a wall. 'Well,' I said, 'I'll have to find out for myself' – and I moved towards the wall. But he sprang in front of me, saying that behind the wall was an area no one could visit without specific permission from a certain high-ranking magistrate. Trying to hide my excitement at the turn of events, I asked him to call the magistrate at once and ask for authorization. He hesitated, spoke agitatedly to the judge on his walkie-talkie, and then said the man wished to receive us all in his office. Naturally, I refused to allow the whole delegation to leave the police station; some of us remained standing at strategic points with instructions not to move on any account. I left, with one colleague and an interpreter, and was driven in a police car to the magistrate's headquarters.

By this time it was two in the afternoon, and we were all exhausted and hungry. But events had taken such a dramatic turn we had to forget our hunger and tiredness.

The magistrate turned out to be short and fat, with an air of great intelligence and guile. We had an animated discussion. He asserted we had no right to visit parts of the building that were off limits to strangers. I contradicted his every statement and concluded that, if he persisted in blocking our inspection, we would have to take the necessary steps at an international level. I got the distinct impression he was unmoved by our threat. Perhaps, though, he was impressed by our obstinacy, as well as by our punctilious criticism of his remarks. So, with a Cheshire cat smile, he said again he thought we were wrong, but out of respect for such 'eminent foreign experts', he would allow our inspection to go forward. He then rang the police inspector in our presence to tell him we were authorized to visit the 'forbidden' rooms.

Another couple of hours had gone by. We were driven back to the police station, found our colleagues worn out by their vigil, but happy to hear the good news. Several police officers removed the secret wall, which lay behind the fire extinguishers. What we found was a tiny door leading to a vast area, with numerous cells, somewhat suspect toilet facilities, and areas used for interrogation. Our police inspector did not look very embarrassed – on the contrary he was quite haughty and spoke again with loud and ostentatious cordiality. He told us that in fact the area had not been used for ten years. This was easy to disprove: not only did we find traces of the rooms and toilets having been used recently, but newspapers from a couple of years earlier and, in some cells, graffiti that had been made a few months, or even days, earlier. In three or four tiny, empty cells there was an unmistakable human smell – proof of very recent occupation – to which a member of our delegation, an expert in penitentiaries, drew our attention (a faint body odour which is left behind when a small room has been occupied for twenty-four hours or more, an odour that lingers on for a couple of days, especially when the ventilation is poor). Thus, although there were no inmates, we found unmistakable indicators that people had been held there a day, or perhaps even a few hours, earlier. We conducted our inspection in minute detail, throughout the area, collected various exhibits – under the speechless and stupefied gaze of the policemen surrounding us – and towards evening we went back to our hotel.

Putting our powers of inspection into practice

To give an adequate idea of how wide-ranging the Committee's powers of inspection are and of how we used them (and my Strasbourg colleagues still use them), a few examples may be worth mentioning.

One afternoon, during our visit to a large jail in a medium-sized country, we began to inspect the punishment unit. This was where prisoners who had broken the prison regulations were shut up, for varying periods of time. On speaking to the inmates, we were told that in one of the cells there had been a boy with a badly bruised face; at dawn, without warning, he had been taken off, and no one knew where he was. With difficulty, after poring through the registers and talking to both the prisoners and the warders of that sector, we discovered the boy's name. But when we asked where he was, we were given very evasive answers. It became more and more obvious they did not want us to talk to him. Fearing he might be transferred to another penitentiary, we asked to see the governor; but it was late, he had already gone home and we were unable to get in touch with him. His deputy, saying he did not have the data we were asking for – most unlikely in our view – suggested we come back the next day. Instead, we marched over to the infirmary, called all the doctors and nurses together, and asked for the immediate presence of the head of the medical department (he too was at home, but we made him come back). We had followed this procedure because we had hoped to find some trace of the lad in the infirmary and then, perhaps, reconstruct his movements. After a few hours, surrounded by irritated doctors and nurses, we got the details we needed, including the boy's medical certificates – which mentioned multiple bruises, but not what had caused them. After further conversations we discovered the boy could only be in one of two wards, unless he had been taken out of the prison altogether. We divided into two subgroups, each going at once to one ward. It was now midnight, and the inmates were asleep when we arrived. The welcome the warders gave us was hardly friendly. After half an hour of questions and going from cell to cell we discovered the cell where the boy had been put. We woke him and his cell mate and, having received his consent, we questioned him at length, and had him examined by our own doctor. It transpired that the lad had gone to the infirmary to be examined by one of the prison doctors and had lost his patience at the total indifference of the latter (who had kept him waiting for over an hour for no apparent reason), had beaten his fists on the table and brandished a large book; the doctor, fearing attack, had called for help; three warders had come in, punched and kicked the boy, before the doctor's eyes; the latter had then applied a couple of band-aids to the bruises, given him an injection of tranquillizer, and had then sent him off to the punishment unit. We drafted a summary report on his bruises, swollen face and one black eye. The next day we held separate interviews with the doctor and the prison governor. The doctor was young and fairly inexperienced; he confirmed part of the boy's account, but said he had not seen the warders beat him up, because he had been writing out a certificate; he felt the boy had got his black eye by knocking into a piece of

furniture in his surgery. Our own doctor – with many
years' experience of working in prisons – had no difficulty
in confuting these statements.

Do not imagine, however, that in exercising our powers
of investigation we always achieved results or confirmed
our suspicions, or always caught the authorities at deviant
or oppressive behaviour. Occasionally, we followed false
trails, or were deliberately led astray, if not almost cheated
by some officials. Let me give a few examples of this, too.

In one police station with its ground floor partly occupied by cells for terrorist suspects we were told, towards
the end of our inspection, that the inmates could often
hear shrieks and moans coming either from the floor above
or from the one below. Sometimes they could hear the
noise of many footsteps, of furniture and heavy objects
being moved, followed at once by screams and groans.
During our two days of inspection throughout the very
large ground floor we had never heard of such things, and
had felt certain that the rest of the building (which
apparently only had one other floor) contained offices. We
decided to make further investigations. We soon discovered that the basement was used as storage space, full
of discarded objects and exhibits; there was no room for
interrogating or torturing a suspect there. We determined
to go up to the first floor. But at this point the head officer
refused to let us do so; he said that floor contained no
detainees and no interrogation rooms, only staff and
objects covered by military secrecy. Access was prohibited
to anyone, even the military, except for the intelligence
services. We stuck our ground: we had a right to visit any
part of a building where there were people deprived of
their liberty. He again refused. We then had an animated
and unpleasant altercation, made worse by the officer's
being extremely tall, with hard blue eyes and all the
aggressiveness of a martinet. Besides, as soon as we began
our discussion, we were literally surrounded by dozens of

policemen. The giant refused to give me his name and rank (which I needed for a report on the incident). His behaviour made me more and more suspicious and I tried another tack, asking to speak to his superior.

A police car took us to see this high-ranking official. The ensuing discussion was far from serene. I countered his refusal to give us access by pointing out that state officials could only defer our visits – and only for reasons of national defence and public safety – but that we would, in any case, be allowed to visit those premises sooner or later, to verify whether our information on their use for detention purposes was accurate. I insisted on speaking to the ministerial authorities, to inform them we would be making an official protest and, if necessary, that we would put an end to our inspection and leave the country. Egged on by our obduracy, the man telephoned his superiors in the ministry. A long conversation was followed by his offer to have us taken round that first floor, though only after the staff had evacuated it and on condition we did not look too closely at certain special equipment they kept there. He explained that the floor was occupied by a special anti-terrorist unit, hence we must not see the faces of its members, nor the sophisticated apparatus they used. We had to accept these conditions, even though we suspected them to be mere pretexts, and that the lapse of time would be used to remove any detainees.

An hour later we returned to the police station and went up to the first floor. On careful scrutiny we were satisfied that the empty rooms could not be used to detain or interrogate prisoners, for a series of practical reasons that we put to the test; moreover the furniture and other objects, the arms and the equipment we glimpsed, confirmed the version given us by the authorities. We thanked the giant, excused ourselves for the upset, explaining that we had merely been exercising our rights; our information had, indeed, proved inaccurate, but it had been our duty to ascertain its veracity. However, since the detainee who had given us this information seemed credible, two days later we went back to the police station and went over the ground floor. Having questioned a new inmate who had been brought in the previous evening, we tried to find out if our informer had been wrong, and if so, why. We made a couple of experiments (one of us went into an empty cell close to that of the informer and two others went into the interrogation rooms nearby, closed the double doors, and shouted out several times, varying the tone and volume of our cries). It thus seemed plausible that a person in one of the cells might hear the cries coming from one of the two rooms – a somewhat muffled sound in any case – and think they came from the floors below or above.

As I have already said, in some cases the authorities led us astray, quite deliberately. On one occasion, in an overcrowded prison, one of the inmates of a vast dormitory told us, in front of the other detainees, that he had been beaten up, more than once, in a given police station. He gave us a precise description of the building, of the very unhealthy, dirty cells, of the utensils the police used to ill-treat prisoners. Another inmate who was listening – and had been detained in the same police station – added other details. In the end we had enough evidence to recognize the police station. We went there a few hours later. We were immediately received by a smiling, affable officer who, far from putting off our visit as we had expected, took us round at once. Everything was spic and span. The cells were empty and the carefully kept registers seemed credible. Although the premises corresponded exactly to the description we had been given by the prisoners, they were in perfect trim and there was no sign of the instruments that had been described. We realized there was no use staying on and we left our police inspector, who smiled smugly as he shook hands. On returning to our hotel we concluded that some of the prisoners must have been police informers, who had deliberately given us false information both to make a nonsense of our work and waste our precious time. One of our group suggested another line, which seemed less probable: the prisoners had been sincere, but another inmate, with contacts in the police, had given warning of our impending visit, so the police station had been cleaned up and prepared for us. In any case that particular visit was a notable fiasco.

The impact of inspectors

So far I have tried to illustrate how we exercised our fact-finding powers and the difficulties into which we ran. I shall now turn to our main concern: once the facts have been collected and an evaluation made, what do the inspectors do to stop ill-treatment or to put an end to inhuman and degrading conditions? Above all, what can be done to prevent such things occurring in future?

Our first 'intervention' can take place at the end of a visit, before we leave the country. The inspectors have the right to present their first impressions and remarks ('immediate observations') to the government authorities, suggesting measures to be taken with some urgency. This was done more than once, with very good results. To give an example, during a visit to a prison in Switzerland we found two people detained in a unit comprising two 'security and meditation cells', reserved for violent or dangerous prisoners, or for those with suicidal tendencies. The two prisoners were naked and in a state of grave mental confusion. The cells, which were dark and squalid, had only a faint ray of natural light seeping through a tiny opening. On the cement floor was a raised cement platform with a foam-rubber mattress. Each cell had two doors, one a steel grill. A video camera kept an eye on the inmates. The inspectors found that these conditions were not fit for any human being, and certainly not for people suffering from mental illness. The Swiss authorities sent an inspector of their own at once and, having ascertained the conditions of the cells, transferred the two prisoners to other institutions and then made the necessary improvements.

In Switzerland again, the Strasbourg inspectors found two fairly large cells in the 'prison area' of a police station, full of foreigners. The cells were dirty and unhealthy, with no natural source of light, and practically no ventilation. Most of the inmates had been there for over a week: day in, day out. Again the inspectors found the cells were unfit for human habitation. After a couple of weeks the Swiss authorities let us know they had evacuated the premises, begun work on a radical reconstruction of the rooms and built new cells. The same occurred in many other cases: the authorities of other countries (such as France) got in touch at once to say that the cells the Committee had inspected had either been withdrawn from service, or radically transformed, or else that they were making inquiries about the police officers in the stations we had described as being at risk, or had started disciplinary or criminal proceedings against them.

The most revealing case occurred in a country we visited more than once. On the first visit, the inspectors made some devastating criticisms of one police station, because it had tiny, suffocating cells. Soon afterwards the government began construction of a new building. When, on the next visit, the inspectors saw that this building also had some severe drawbacks (the builders having reached the first floor) they asked the government to demolish the walls and redraft the plans. This time the government followed our advice to the letter. Thus, on the third visit, the inspectors saw that the new building (now completed) was adequate; in particular, the detention cells had been completely rebuilt and satisfied the standards laid down two years earlier.

Apart from passing on such immediate observations, what does the work of the Committee involve? After careful discussion of the results of their inquiries, the inspectors submit a confidential report to the government concerned. Here they not only present their conclusions, but also make suggestions on modifications they deem necessary. These suggestions range far and wide: from the rights of people held in police custody to conditions in detention cells; from overcrowding in prisons to family visits and access to a lawyer; from work opportunities to recreation facilities in prisons, as well as medical services in all detention centres, and so on. A vast range of situations and conditions have to be covered, for which the Committee does not refrain from making recommendations that will affect the activities of the legislature, the judiciary and the administration of a given state. These recommendations do not pile up in dusty files. The recipient state is expected to respond within six months and a year later, to give details of how they have been implemented; should this not have been altogether possible, it must report on the reasons why the Committee's recommendations could not all be put into effect. If the Committee is not satisfied, it may decide to carry out another visit in the same country, or merely reiterate its criticisms, comments and recommendations. To these the state must give an answer, within a fixed time-limit determined by the Committee.

This is how an intense dialogue is set up with each country we visit, and this makes it difficult for the state to disregard our recommendations. Thus, after each visit a sort of ping-pong match begins between the state capital and Strasbourg. To put it differently, Strasbourg exerts continuous and effective pressure to make each government introduce the changes and improvements which will end an intolerable situation, or prevent risky conditions from degenerating.

If this dialogue breaks down, because the state is either reluctant or unable to make the changes the inspectors requested, then the latter have only one weapon left: they can seek the attention of public opinion by making that 'public statement' mentioned in chapter 2. This is the only form of sanction the Committee can apply, but the knowledge that it will use it – with all the negative consequences this may have on the state at an international level – has a considerable deterrent effect. That is why the Committee has, so far, only made one such 'statement', about Turkey, and only after various inspections to that country, followed by reports and an intense exchange of comments and responses. The reverberations of the statement in the press and on public opinion, together with the effect it may have on the decisions of other international bodies (such as the European Union) make it possible to hope that the situation in Turkey will slowly improve.

Apart from Turkey, what has been the real effect of the Committee's recommendations? As I have said, despite instances of unwillingness, most states have always given instant effect to the inspectors' immediate observations. Little by little, governments are also implementing the general recommendations contained in the Strasbourg Committee's reports. Over all, things are going fairly well, even though gigantic problems still loom and it is not possible to resolve them quickly.

Proof of the good effect of the inspections is the fact that many states have decided to publish the reports made on their system of detention. Despite the harsh criticism they contain, governments have chosen to make these strictures and recommendations public. By so doing they have waived the only right they preserved under the

Convention: the right to keep the results of the Committee's inspections secret. This attitude, which is more and more prevalent, does not only confirm how conscientious, scrupulous and impartial the inspectors' work has been, but proves how the democratic governments of Europe have determined to become as transparent as glass-houses, even in the most obscure and hidden corners of their state administrations. Hence, states eventually endow the inspectors' work with a *pedagogic* value that had not been foreseen by the Convention's drafters. The inspectors' report on a given state, once published, opens the eyes of ordinary people to a little-known subject and informs other states about what goes on in that country. Besides, both the people and the governments of Europe form an idea of the criteria by which to judge these hidden 'human dustbins', which still litter our continent. Above all, the reports show how these dustbins can be made less inhuman, together with what changes and improvements should be aimed at in each specific case.

5

What Is Human, Inhuman or Degrading?

When we were in Strasbourg drafting the international Convention that was to set up the Committee, we wondered if we should define the standards the future inspectors would need to gauge the detention centres they visited: in other words, whether we should spell out the precise meaning of 'torture' and 'inhuman or degrading' treatment or punishment. Many thought we should not send the inspectors off into the unknown without instructions on what was to be regarded as blameworthy or acceptable in the behaviour of states. Without a compass, how could they find their way through the tortuous labyrinth of human affairs they were about to traverse? – such was the opinion of some state representatives. But when we sat down to define these concepts we found it very hard to reach an agreement. One of us reminded the others of that wise and hoary maxim of the Roman jurist Javolenus that any definition is dangerous, because it can easily be subverted (*omnis definitio in iure civili periculosa est: parum est enim ut non subverti posset*). After much racking of brains and lengthy discussion we gave it up. The inspectors would have to work out their own rules of navigation, guided by their expertise, common sense and experience.

It was a wise decision. From the very beginning of our work, we never felt the lack of general principles or criteria. We thought we must proceed along pragmatic lines, each case requiring specific parameters on which to base an evaluation of the concrete situation we had before us. In several years of work, face to face with a specific situation, we hardly ever entertained strong doubts: it was either acceptable, or not at all. Looking back, I am surprised how there was never any major disagreement among us, whatever our respective nationality and profession: whether we came from Northern, Southern or Central Europe, or from Asiatic countries such as Turkey and Cyprus; whether we were doctors, lawyers, psychiatrists, psychologists, experts in penitentiary systems, former members of parliament – we always saw the situations we were expected to evaluate in the same light, as 'human' or 'inhuman'. This goes to prove, without a tremor of doubt, that the citizens of Europe, at least, share a common perception of such matters. (Besides, as early as 1764, Cesare Beccaria had already said: 'Let us consult our hearts, and there we shall find the fundamental principles.' These principles embraced contractualism and utilitarianism – as advocated by Locke, Rousseau and Helvetius – not to mention the earlier tenets and maxims of the Gospels, none of which have been lost with the passing of centuries, but have become embedded in European culture.)

But – you might object – how did we recognize, with such self-assurance and unanimity, what is unendurable? What is the litmus paper that transforms an 'acceptable' situation into one that is reprehensible and to be condemned? As I said in chapter 3, our job was to prevent both torture and inhuman or degrading treatment or punishment. To prevent, we agreed, meant that it would not be enough to identify and condemn the conditions, treatment or punishment that are repugnant to one's sense of humanity. To prevent means to identify all such situations as are on the verge of becoming unendurable, in other words all those situations that belong to that dingy area of human behaviour which could so easily degenerate into the inhuman. Hence our mandate included not only a search for the obviously intolerable, but also for any behaviour that could, quickly or slowly, degenerate into the inhuman. At first this seemed an impossible task; in fact it proved to be less difficult once we began our work with all the thoroughness and rigour it required.

Having mapped out the field of our activities, we then had to find out that situations merited the tag *hic sunt leones*: that shadowy area we intended to penetrate. Thus, it was easy to establish our first solid point of reference: the exact meaning of 'torture'. Here we were helped by history, by the great writers of the Enlightenment (Verri, Beccaria, Voltaire), by recent books (for instance, *La question* by Henri Alleg on the war in Algeria, or *The Confession* by Artur London, in which this Czech politician described the horrible methods used by the intelligence services in his country to torture political dissidents in the 1950s). We were also greatly helped by the decisions of the European Court of Human Rights (such as the one on the so-called techniques for helping in interrogation, used by the British in Northern Ireland, or the report by the European Commission of Human Rights on Greece under the colonels). Without any discussion among ourselves, we agreed that torture was any form of coercion or violence, whether mental or physical, against a person to extort a confession, information, or to humiliate, punish or intimidate that person. In all cases of torture, inhuman treatment is deliberate: one person behaves towards another in such a way as to hurt body or mind, and to offend that person's sense of dignity. In other words, torture is intended to humiliate, offend and degrade a human being and turn him or her into a 'thing'.

The cases of torture we encountered were a cruel confirmation of the general concepts we had in mind when we began our work. Naturally, we never caught a policeman or a jailer in the act of perpetrating cruelty and violence: it takes only a couple of minutes to whisk tools of torture out of sight and to take the victims elsewhere. No international inspector, however smart and however impromptu his visit, can expect to catch the bureaucrats of violence in the act of tormenting the mind and body of a victim. However, it is easy to discover physical and even psychological traces of torture – these we came across quite frequently in a few countries, as I shall describe in my next chapter. Occasionally, it is also possible, if one acts very fast, to chance upon the instruments of torture.

It is more difficult to discover 'inhuman' or 'degrading' situations. First, because, unlike torture, which takes the form of single acts against an individual, these situations are the result of numerous acts and circumstances combined. They are often caused by the cumulative effect of the behaviour of many different persons. Second, in cases of 'inhuman' or 'degrading' treatment, the intent to humiliate, offend or debase the victim is almost always absent. Although such situations are, in effect, contrary to one's sense of what is human, it is often hard to discern a malevolent purpose in the perpetrators. Yet, despite these difficulties, we never harboured serious doubts, once we were faced by concrete situations.

Little by little we ended up classifying what we saw into three loose categories:

(1) situations that are not intrinsically unacceptable, but which could become so, either because they *combine with other factors*, or because they can *degenerate* (I gave examples of this in chapter 3: the 'human parking lot'; or a person held in custody being prevented from exercising any of the four fundamental rights mentioned above; or

again, the practice of some policemen of blindfolding a person they are questioning);

(2) situations that are *inadmissible* because they are not compatible with the concept of respect for the basic human rights of the individual;

(3) situations that are *inhuman or degrading*.

The difference between categories (2) and (3), which are not meant to be based on rigorously scientific distinctions but merely on operative criteria, is one of gravity and degree: sometimes we came across conditions of detention that, though unacceptable, were not such as could be described as utterly repugnant to our sense of human dignity.

Let me give some examples, starting with situations we considered inhuman or degrading. In more than one country, for example the United Kingdom, the following conditions were seen: each cell contains two or three inmates, accommodated in a very cramped space; there is no sign of sanitary installations (each prisoner has a bucket, to be used in front of the others; the collective toilet facilities may be used twice a day and for emptying the bucket); there are no regime activities (work, education, vocational training, sport, etc.); the prisoners spend about twenty-two hours out of twenty-four in their cells. Who can deny that the combination of overcrowding, lack of integral sanitation and the absence of regime activities indeed amount to a form of inhuman and degrading treatment?

When we found such conditions, we did not hesitate one second in defining them as contrary to the principles of humane treatment. Take the lack of sanitary arrangements. Since childhood we have been brought up to satisfy the needs of nature alone; to do so in front of others is deeply humiliating, both for ourselves and for the others. It is equally humiliating, for all, to have to slop out one's bucket many hours after having used it. Yet all this becomes quite unbearable when people are forced to live one on top of the other, in an enclosed and cramped space, for almost a day and a night. If these prisoners could spend most of the day outside the cell, working, doing exercise, practising a sport, following courses in vocational training, the fact of sharing such a small space with two or three other inmates would be less intolerable, and it would be less degrading not to have individual toilet facilities attached to the cell. Thus we came to the conclusion that the pernicious combination of these three factors constituted, without a shadow of doubt, inhuman and degrading treatment. I cannot get the faces of the many young men I saw in such prisons out of my mind. Even those who had spent only a few days in these brutalizing conditions had the opaque gaze of men with no future. They answered our questions willingly, but never smiled, all the more so since they realized we could do nothing to help them individually.

Nor did we entertain any doubt in considering repugnant the cells we visited in numerous police stations in various countries: they were so small that it was impossible to stretch out on the floor, the choice being between standing, and crouching in a foetal position in order to sit down. They were usually ill-lit (a faint ray of daylight came through a small round hole up high, just under the ceiling) and they almost invariably stank of urine or excrement. Once, on finding an empty cell, I stepped in and closed the heavy metal door, to find out for myself what it felt like to be shut in there. After a few minutes I had to beat on the door to be let out. I told my psychiatrist colleague, who was standing talking to a guard in the corridor, that if I had been shut up in one of those cells, I would have gone mad after a few hours. He smiled and said that I could have borne it for many hours before giving in to the black dog of depression; more than a whole day was necessary to go out of one's mind. These cells, which in our private jargon we called 'coffins', are used in some countries for people held in custody for a week or more.

Similarly, nobody will dispute that cells – such as we saw in many police stations – are inhuman if the detainee is kept in total darkness for the whole period of detention. In some countries this can be longer than a week. Once I entered one of these cells to question the inmate, a man suspected of having committed terrorist attacks. The door was opened and he rose from a makeshift pallet; he was about forty, lean and skinny and came towards us respectfully, covering his eyes because he had been blinded by the sudden flood of light from the corridor. His clothes were very shabby and blue-black stubble, several days old, adorned his chin. He indicated the cell and excused himself for not offering either a stool or a bed for us to sit on (indeed, apart from the pallet, a dark blanket and a sort of bowl with a piece of bread in it, there was absolutely nothing else). I asked him if he was willing to speak to us and answer a few questions. He nodded. For the whole exchange we stood in semi-darkness. When I asked him how long he had spent in that cell, he said he did not know, because he had been unable to count the days: spending several days and nights in complete darkness had made him lose his sense of time. But he did not complain: he was often able to guess the beginning of a new day by the corridors becoming noisier and by the increased number of voices of policemen he could hear.

In some countries I visited police stations which held various types of detainee, such as foreigners awaiting deportation, people suspected of common crimes, convicts with very short sentences. Some stayed there no more than a day, but most detainees were held for a week and some for as long as a month. The premises were dark, depressing and unhealthy, and there was nothing to do except leave one's cell to go to the toilet, or walk up and down the corridor. In one country there was the added luxury of being able to stand a while in front of a television set. Never – not even for a quarter of an hour – were the detainees allowed outside, never was there any sport or recreation: just inertia and hebetude.

I do not wish to carry on with this sequence of horrors, but some other examples, chosen at random from my notebooks, seem equally instructive.

Take, for example, the case of the young prisoner I met on his arrival in a high-security prison. I was with one of our doctors and an interpreter, and decided to start asking questions at once, while he was unpacking: I wanted to know about conditions in the prison he had just left. He was a big twenty-six year old lad, good-looking, but rather downcast. As soon as he started to answer my questions, to our great surprise we noticed he had lost almost all his teeth. We forgot our questions on the other prison and asked how he had become virtually toothless. He told us he had spent four years in various prisons, that he had all his teeth (only one broken tooth), and that decay had taken them off one by one; this was because the prison dentists did not cure them, but pulled them out (once they had extracted seven at a sitting); now, at twenty-six, he was left with only five teeth out of thirty-two (a canine and four incisors). His story struck us as so incredible that we decided to check his medical file, talked to the prison authorities, inquired whether he suffered from some specific illness (such as pyorrhoea or gingivitis) that could cause loss of teeth, but we found nothing. What transpired was that in that country – which was neither poor nor underdeveloped – the prison authorities did not provide dental care for prisoners: toothache was cured by removing the offending tooth. As a result, in the case of our young man, the prisoner was forced to eat nothing but mushy food like a baby, and to mumble like an old man, without any hope of improving his situation, partly because he was serving a long sentence, partly because he did not have the money to buy false teeth. Could anyone doubt the young man had been treated in an inhuman manner?

Conditions equally repugnant to our sense of human dignity we found in one of the most civilized countries: France. When a prisoner there has to be transferred to a civil hospital for specialist care, or even for medical care that is impossible in prison, he is adequately guarded by police officers, and is usually handcuffed or otherwise tied up. There have therefore been cases of women prisoners who have given birth while handcuffed to their beds. We could not believe this to be true, so we tried to discover the logic of the procedure that led to such absurd results. The police officers we questioned admitted quite candidly that they were duty-bound to comply with police regulations, which require, as a safety precaution, that a detainee must be handcuffed, to avoid any chance of escape during transfer. When we pointed out that a woman who is in labour is not likely to run away, the policemen shrugged and said it was up to a doctor to take responsibility for removing the woman's handcuffs (I must add that, when the French authorities received our report, they ordered an immediate and very thorough inquiry, and subsequently put an end to such aberrant practice).

We found a similar state of affairs in another country, where we learnt on irreproachable authority that a woman prisoner, who had given birth in a hospital under police surveillance, had had the baby removed a few minutes later (the child had been given to foster parents). The visiting delegation of our Committee found that the mother-child couple had been subjected to flagrantly inhuman treatment.

No less mortifying was what we saw in one big prison, in the section reserved for family visits. So that the prison guards could keep an eye on these encounters, above all to prevent prisoners from receiving any drugs, along the opposite walls of a large room, at a distance of four metres, panels of wood or opaque plastic had been erected to form a kind of horse box; on one side was the wall, the panels made up two other sides, while the fourth was open and gave on to a central corridor. The guards walked up and down between the two rows of boxes and could easily keep an eye on the prisoners. By tacit agreement, even though it was implicitly forbidden by law, the prisoners were allowed to make love to their partners. As a result this love making went on under the eyes not only of the guards, but of other inmates being visited by their families, including many children who were running around, in and out of the boxes. It is hard to imagine a more degrading situation, not only for the prisoners themselves, who were forced to copulate furiously like animals, but also for their fellow inmates who were being visited by their families and were witnessing these scenes, not to mention the prison guards, obliged to play the shameful role of voyeurs. We pointed out to the prison governor that such situations may easily lead to warders blackmailing prisoners. The poor man sighed his agreement. The hypocrisy of the prison regulations did not explicitly forbid such sexual encounters; nor did they explicitly consent to their taking place, in suitable premises, for an adequate period of time, as one moment within the wider context of a loving relationship.

I cannot end this thumbnail sketch of inhuman situations without mentioning a practice that is very widespread, especially in Northern Europe: solitary confinement. We saw dozens and dozens of prisoners kept in solitary confinement for months on end, and in some cases for years. No doubt in many countries prisoners enjoy all the forms of modern accommodation: a comfortable cell with impeccable sanitary arrangements, a radio, a colour television, newspapers and magazines. Yet they do not have any real social contacts: they can speak only to the guards, or to the doctor when they are ill, and with relatives once or twice a month. They do no work, have no sport, do not attend classes, and never take the air with other prisoners. Perhaps they are being detained on remand and have to be kept separate from other prisoners either for the needs of a criminal investigation or as a security measure. Alternatively, a prisoner who has been sentenced to many years of solitary confinement may well be a dangerous and violent individual, who may have committed extremely serious crimes. But do these reasons justify the progressive suffocation of the prisoners' personality by denying them fundamental human relationships? Why cause their humanity to shrivel, and perhaps to be annulled? Is there any justification for reducing human beings to the state of larvae, where the self is expressed in repetitive physical gestures, until what little, or great, humanity the prisoner possessed on being jailed perishes slowly until it disappears completely?

Let me relate what we saw in the high-security unit of a modern prison in one of the most advanced countries in Europe. This section had numerous cells for dangerous prisoners sentenced for very serious crimes. Only a few of these were inhabited at the time of our visit, and all by men serving life sentences. We went to see a multiple murderer. He was a dark-skinned giant with a bald head: a pigtail of hair descended from his nape to his waist. Perhaps it was this unusual appearance that had earned him the nickname Apache. As soon as he saw us, he asked us to come into the cell and close the door. He was known to be so dangerous that we were rather hesitant (there were only two of us). As he insisted, we went in, wordlessly taking the standard precautions (one stays by the door, and the other between the door and the prisoner, with our eyes never leaving his face for an instant). We understood at once why he had wanted us to shut ourselves in with him. By gestures he indicated we should keep quiet and listen. We could now hear a constant hiss, produced by the air conditioner; after a little, the noise became less intense, as the prisoner indicated with gestures. Apart from the hiss, there was absolutely no other noise. The cell was roomy, with a radio and a television and a small toilet annex. The window, a very large one, had no bars because it was made of shatter-proof glass and could not be opened. All one could see was a very high wall opposite. The murderer was kept in total acoustic isolation. Apart from the low hiss, one might have been buried in a tomb. He pointed out that he always noticed, at once, any variation in the hiss, caused by variation in the electric current, or by some other technical reason. We asked him if he ever spoke to anyone. He saw the guard twice a day; the latter passed him his food through a slit in the wall, which the guard opened by pushing an electronic button in the corridor. He was allowed one shower, and half an hour's 'airing' a day, in a kind of metal cage in the open air, where he could walk up and down, all on his own. When the guard opened the door to take him to the shower or to the cage, they sometimes exchanged a few words. Later, the prison officers told us that the doctor visited him only when it was necessary, the social worker never, because he was afraid of him. The prisoner never saw his relations, because they lived far away in his native land. He had spent five or six years in that cell, ruminating his unhappy thoughts and had no idea whether he would be there for life. He had not yet passed over from the animal to the vegetable kingdom, but we got an idea of his future condition on entering another cell, where the prisoner, who had horribly murdered several people, had been kept for seven years. He lay on his bed, as pale as a ghost, moaning incomprehensible words. The only thing we understood was a faint 'no' when we asked if we were disturbing him and if he preferred to be left alone. He started and trembled at the slightest noise, however imperceptible, which we made while we stayed in the cell. We left soon after.

So far I have described situations the Committee has defined as 'inhuman' or 'degrading'. But, as I have already said, the Committee also recognized a less serious category, of 'inadmissible' situations. Let me now give some examples of this.

More than once the Strasbourg inspectors protested against the custom of keeping people awaiting trial (and therefore presumed innocent) in the same prison as convicts. Furthermore, in some countries the inspectors noted that prisoners were subjected to prolonged periods of disciplinary segregation. In certain prisons they found 'punishment cells' containing minors and adults shut in together. In another case, the Committee found a prisoner who had been awaiting a major operation; the prison authorities had done nothing about the prison doctor's request for almost two years, which had led to serious complications for the man's health. On other occasions, we complained that the prison authorities had refused to allow detainees (they were common criminals) to telephone their families, even though (in the case of foreign prisoners) the latter resided in another country so that visits were hardly ever possible. In each of these and other similar cases, the Committee determined the situations to be unacceptable and requested the relevant state to introduce immediate improvements.

The examples given so far, taken from the various categories of situations we censored, do not represent all the types of problem we encountered. More than once, indeed, we were only able to begin a census of the most common inhuman and degrading situations. Others exist that we barely touched on, or were able to point out without examining them in detail. For instance, some people have to spend very long periods in prison awaiting

trial, months or even years, waiting to be declared innocent or guilty. Is this not a form of unjustifiable suffering?
Or take prisoners who are terminally ill with cancer or
Aids: when their families or a health service institution are
willing to look after them, why should they spend the
remainder of their days in a cell? Finally, the extenuating
length of time during which foreigners asking for asylum
are often held in internment camps. How can one alleviate
the state of anguish and uncertainty in which they wait?

Another issue we hardly touched on was the role of sex
in prisons. Perhaps our first visits were so overwhelmed by
far more complex and serious problems that we unconsciously set it aside, as if it were of minor importance. It
was a subject we came across only in two countries, where
we were faced by specific and unacceptable situations: I
have already referred to one, with couples making love
furiously in the visiting hours, in front of dozens of people,
some of them children; the other was in a country that
allows each prisoner two hours' 'conjugal visits' a month.
Although we approved this open-mindedness by the authorities, we were forced to criticize the circumstances in
which these visits took place: partners were frisked all over
beforehand, justifiable as a prevention of drug smuggling,
but humiliating for the person concerned; the rooms in
which these encounters took place were fairly squalid; and
above all, only certain hours on certain days were set aside
for these visits, depriving them of any affective content
and reducing them to mere outbursts of sex. On this
occasion the Committee took the opportunity to suggest
the construction of proper buildings, within the prison
walls, for meetings between prisoners and their families,
to allow family units to spend a whole day together fairly
frequently (though another possibility, for prisoners not
considered dangerous, was to be sent home for a few days,
at least once a month).

Although the Committee was barely able to touch on

such issues as I have just mentioned, obviously such manifestations of inhuman behaviour, especially in places of detention, need to be scrutinized at length; and the efforts of the Strasbourg inspectors to prevent them, or iron them out, must continue.

Whatever the results of our explorations, I think one can agree on one essential point, which I would like to go over again. I feel the cases I have mentioned are proof of how relatively easy it is to size up a situation as being intolerable. One needs only to apply those 'principles of humane conduct' embedded in our culture. I am thinking in particular, of the Enlightenment and rationalism. Admittedly, rationalism, in one specific aspect, may have contributed to the birth of great barbarity, including concentration camps (as was pointed out by Adorno and Horkheimer, though, in fact, they were reacting against a particular form of rationalism). However, it also brought forth certain values and ethical principles that have been of first importance. Joseph de Maistre was wrong when, in 1797, he wrote: 'There is no such thing as man in this world. In my life, I have come across Frenchmen, Italians, Russians; thanks to Montesquieu, I also know that there are Persians; as for *man*, I can declare I have never met him in my life; if he does exist, it is beyond my ken.' In all modesty, I feel we did meet 'man'. Often this was 'negative man'. But we were able to discern and condemn any negation of humane behaviour precisely because each one of us carried within a clear idea of 'man' and 'humanity'. Many of us had never read Pascal, Rousseau, Beccaria or Kant. Yet, we were all moved by the same concepts and applied the same criteria.

All very well, you may object, yet why did this concept of human dignity not inspire the doctors who allowed a woman to give birth in chains, or who did not treat the teeth of a poor young man when these were rotting away in his mouth? Why does it not affect the police who, day

59

after day, open and close the doors to those tiny cells in which, perhaps, not even an animal could survive? Why is there no trace of it in the prison officers who guard the cells where human larvae spend their days in complete and abject solitude? Why does it not influence warders working in overcrowded prisons, with no proper sanitation, in which prisoners spend their time in craven and brutish sloth?

The only answer I can give is tentative and uncertain (who would dare suggest definitive answers to such fathomless and complicated issues?). My answer is that the concept of humanity, just like that of human rights, is not innate. As the French biologist and essayist Jean Hamburger remarked so wisely, there is nothing so false as to suppose that human rights are 'natural', that is innate. Rather the contrary is true. Our biological nature causes us to overpower – not to respect – our fellows, to assert our individuality – not to express solidarity. If it is true that each one of us contains a fragment of the Divine, it is also true that the 'brimstone' element prevails. To put it in non-religious terms: even the most enlightened individual is torn between a biological ego (which encourages a tendency to overwhelm others) and a social ego (which should soften and sweeten these violent impulses).

If this is so, it takes very little to weaken or blunt that concept of human dignity which, notwithstanding, survives in the outstanding principles of European culture. If there are unsatisfactory standards of living, if sound social and cultural models are lacking, if a belief – perhaps unconscious – in irrational values and ideologies prevails (racism, nationalism, a hatred of aliens and so on): all these can induce a doctor, a policeman, a prison officer, a magistrate, to resort to or to tolerate the inhuman and degrading treatment of others.

My conclusion will seem obvious: the struggle to make the principles of humanity prevail must be carried on day after day; it is the wearisome labour of Sysiphus, which none of us should shirk. In the words of the French writer Vercors, humanity is 'a form of dignity that must be won', a 'painful dignity' that can be won only 'at the cost of many tears'.

6

On Torture

'Give me a little piece of skin and I'll stick hell into it', are the words Hemingway placed in the mouth of a torturer. That is exactly it: torture is hell in a person's body or mind. It is a form of hell that has accompanied our civilization: a German psychoanalyst rightly pointed out that even the image of the crucifix – such an integral part of Western culture – while symbolizing redemption, is above all an image of punishment through torture.

New forms of torture

Do not imagine that medieval torments are still applied, using those horrific instruments we can view in museums – such as can still be seen in the small, squat building of the Gevangenpoort, hidden away just opposite the Dutch Parliament in The Hague. Possibly, in other parts of the world such antiquated methods are still applied; not in Europe. With us methods have become more subtle and sophisticated: the torturers have become more artful and have learnt to torment their victims without leaving any trace. Why has this change taken place? I think there are two main, interconnected reasons.

In the modern age, public opinion has gradually learnt to appreciate human dignity as a supreme good, something that must be respected. The concept became rooted in our consciousness way back in the late eighteenth century and was slowly incorporated into the constitutions of Western democracies; in 1948 it was raised to its present position as a supranational value, when the Universal Declaration of Human Rights was written to sweep away the misdeeds of the Nazi period and solemnly proclaim certain principles as valid for all humankind, in the hope that no one would ever neglect them again. One consequence of these developments is that certain dreadful forms of behaviour that demean a person's humanity are now prohibited and considered absolutely reprehensible. Torture, like genocide, racial discrimination and despotism in all its forms, is now a *negative value*. Not that we have suddenly stopped committing such crimes. But anyone who tramples essential human rights underfoot is fully aware of perpetrating a dreadful deed and shattering a social taboo. More important – and this is the second reason – such taboos have been incorporated into penal law; they have become legal prescriptions that state administrations (in the persons of police, judges and prison officers) must obey and enforce with all the authority a modern state has at its disposal. In short: torture is now dangerous for whosoever is caught red-handed.

Torturers have learnt to adapt. Gone are the wheels, knotted ropes, trestles bristling with steel points, together with other complex and ingenious mechanisms. In a sense torture has become more domestic and unpretentious. But no less painful. Let me give you a rapid sketch of the more common forms: those, at least, we came across in our inspections.

One very widespread form consists in insistently beating the soles of the prisoner's feet or the palms of the hands with a stick or a truncheon. This is much used in

Mediterranean countries, especially Turkey (it has also been used – though quite rarely – in such countries as Italy, as can be seen from certain recent decisions of Italian courts). It has a name: *fàlaka* or *falanga*. Why is it so widely practised? Because the necessary tools are to be found lying around any police station. Besides, it is very effective (pain in these sensitive areas is intense), but traces of the torture can soon be made to disappear: in some countries the detainee is forced to jump up and down barefoot in a few centimetres of water, or to walk up and down for an hour or more in the interrogation room, until the swelling goes down: otherwise anti-inflammatory cream is spread on the hands or feet. Sometimes, according to some prisoners, when there is no medication, yoghurt is used instead. After a couple of days, that is when the detainees are usually released by the police or transferred to a prison, it is almost impossible – except for the expert eye – to perceive the swelling.

Another technique, which is less widespread though equally 'economical', is to put a boiling egg under the victim's armpit and then press as hard as possible, despite the wretch's yells. On a couple of occasions, one of our doctors – a surgeon specializing in burns – had no trouble in discovering the cause of the oval burns under the armpit of a detainee, inflicted only one or two weeks earlier.

Another method, which uses even more 'innocent' devices, consists in beating the victim repeatedly over the head with a telephone directory, until the person is stunned, feels dizzy or faints. A more ferocious form of torture, using an equally inoffensive implement, is to put the victim's head in a plastic bag, such as those normally used for rubbish collecting, and to tie it around the neck: a few seconds later there is no more oxygen in the bag and the person begins to suffocate (not a few prisoners told us that as they were about to faint, they tried to bite the bag to tear a hole in it and breathe).

A particularly 'economical' form of torment is to take the victim's clothes off and squirt freezing water at the body with a garden hose. Equally 'economical' is a method used in several countries: prisoners are made to stand against a wall for many hours on end; when they collapse, the guards rush up and make them stand again; lack of rest, of sleep, of food and being forced to stay in one position only, is a terrible torment even for the strongest person.

Other forms of torture that leave no physical marks are mainly psychological: such as taking the prisoners after arrest to a deserted spot, telling them to run away and threatening to shoot them down; or hurling verbal abuse at them, insulting them and threatening to arrest and rape a relative (wife, mother or sister); or to force a detainee to watch while another is being tortured, or to make one listen to the other's yells and moans.

There are, however, other more violent torments that to a certain extent resemble those of the past. For instance, the prisoner's wrists are tied behind the back and the body is suspended by a rope attached to the wrists from a hook in the wall: after a few minutes the victim will feel unbearable pain in the shoulder-blades, shoulders and wrists (this fairly widespread practice is currently called 'Palestinian hanging'). Otherwise, the arms are tied as on a cross to a wooden bar, suspended between two cupboards, so that the detainee hangs there with out-stretched arms bearing the weight of the whole body. In other cases we investigated, we heard that the victim was tied by the feet and suspended, head down and hooded, from a hook in the ceiling; the head was then put in a metal bucket and this was bashed with a truncheon, to produce not only a booming sound in the head but also a sense of suffocation. In all these cases, as you can see, the instruments of torture were close at hand.

Even more cruel is the use of electric shocks. You will

not find torture chambers full of electric wires, electric machinery and metal beds. Usually, what is used is a small electric generator with very high voltage and low amperes. This is kept in an executive type of briefcase, which can easily be removed. The victim is made to sit or lie down on the floor, or on any kind of bed, and the electrodes are applied to very sensitive parts of the body, where no traces will be left (such as teeth, gums or genitals). Only short shocks are given, to inflict intense pain without provoking a heart attack or burns.

In one country – at least in some towns – the police have started to use objects that can be bought for the personal defence of women. Small battery-run contraptions to be carried in a handbag, which give a shock capable of stunning the aggressor for a short while, very painful if applied to the hands or face. Another implement used in that same country is a short plastic stick, made in Germany: at one end two metal needles give very strong shocks when a button on the handle is pressed. The police apply these sticks to sensitive parts of the victim's body (such as the under-arm, the chest or the neck); the electric shocks are extremely painful and leave tiny black pinpricks on the skin for a few days.

Who practises torture, and why?

It is natural to ask oneself this question and I have done so continuously over the past few years. What I have seen and heard leaves me in no doubt: torture is carried out in the police stations and gendarmeries of certain countries; prison authorities and other state-run detention centres never use such cruel methods.

There is unanimous evidence as to why police and gendarmes in certain countries inflict indescribable torments on detainees: they do so for the purpose of extracting

66

information or confessions. Here the medieval principle that torture is *veritatis indagatio per tormentum* still applies. It is worth noting that, in these countries, it is not only people suspected of political crimes who are subjected to torture, but also people suspected of common crimes: theft, kidnapping, murder, drug trafficking, rape, and so on.

There are various reasons why police officers resort to torture, in these same countries. (I· shall not go into the principal psychological motives: in my *Violence and Law in the Modern Age*, Polity Press, Cambridge (UK), 1988, pp. 121–3, I have already described the important experiments carried out by the American psychologist Stanley Milgram on obedience to the orders of a superior.) In some countries there is a tradition of physical violence, ingrained in society; hence the serious ill-treatment of persons suspected of crime is not seen as the aberrant and abnormal behaviour of a few, but as the – somewhat excessive – expression of a widespread mode of 'interpersonal relations'. This is particularly true of Turkey, where a certain degree of physical violence has, for centuries, been considered acceptable in the family, at school, in barracks. It has been contended that, until as late as 1923, when Kemal Atatürk introduced radical reforms, *fàlaka* (which I have just described) was used in moderation as a normal form of punishment in schools. If you go to Istanbul to visit Topkapi, the sultan's famous residence where he lived with his family, concubines and slaves, you will be taken to visit the eunuchs' rooms, near the entrance; formerly, on the walls hung the wooden sticks they used to practise *fàlaka* on anyone who broke the rigid laws of the harem.

In other European countries, where torture was practised until quite recently and where there are still sporadic cases of ill-treatment and abuse, what prevails is the weight of a very authoritarian past, when inflicting atrocious pain to extract confessions or to punish criminals and political opponents was the norm.

Yet social custom and historical tradition are not sufficient to explain what goes on in some of the countries of Europe. There is another factor: often states do not grant law enforcement officers effective means to gather material evidence and proof (such as sophisticated means for telephone tapping and the bugging of rooms, the use of underground agents, etc.). Nor are they given proper training either in the modern techniques of investigation, the ethics of their profession or even a proper grounding in the law. In one country, where we found frequent instances of torture – mostly against drug traffickers, murderers and other such heinous criminals – I was told, on good authority, the story of a recent case. The police had been informed that a huge load of heroin was about to be 'imported' (the information had come from a rival gang, afraid that the price of drugs would plummet); a large freezer-container lorry was stopped and the heroin found; the lorry-driver insisted he did not know either who had sent or who was to receive the drug, and so could name no names; he was tortured, and confessed all.

Besides, such heinous social ills as terrorism and drug trafficking are condemned so unanimously by the public that any means used against them are considered legitimate. Hence the police often feel it justified and even indispensable to use torture to extract confessions. In some countries such as Great Britain and Italy, isolated cases of serious abuse against persons held for questioning have been part of a climate of tension, a consequence of the fight to put down terrorism and organized crime. In Northern Ireland the tension has been aggravated by long years of civil war; furthermore, until the recent past, there had been a tradition of violence in certain military and paramilitary units that can be traced back to Britain's colonial past and up to the 1960s, when some of these units practised torture in a few African countries. All these facts emerged quite clearly, in 1974, when the European Commission and Court of Human Rights condemned Britain for using the notorious five 'techniques of interrogation' when police questioned suspects in Northern Ireland.

Apart from their being illegal, are these practices 'effective'? Do they extract confessions? I have talked to many people who had been tortured. I reached the conclusion that these methods are especially effective with common criminals (particularly authors of lesser crimes such as theft), if they are either physically or mentally fragile. Many persons sentenced for theft have told me, quite candidly, that after an hour, or less, of torture, they confessed what they had done, in great detail. When people are tortured, they become hostage to their own bodies: they are at the mercy of their nerves' perception of pain. This Cesare Beccaria's penetrating eye saw full well, two centuries ago. One of his main criticisms against the use of torture was related to this specific point. He wrote that the use of torture is a way of ascertaining the truth based on 'the muscles and fibres of a wretch'; if one is strong and puts up with the pain, one is considered innocent; if one is weak and frail, one will talk and be considered guilty. The guilty has good reasons not to confess a crime, because further punishment will be avoided; on the other hand, if the innocent confesses to a crime not committed, he or she is either condemned, or else declared innocent – but having suffered torture, that person has already received an unjust punishment. Thus, torture is very similar to the ancient ordeal (the test of guilt or innocence by subjecting the accused to ordeal by fire or boiling water) because the outcome depends on purely physical and extrinsic facts, such as a person's robust constitution or frail nerves.

During our inspections I received tangible proof of the profound truth in Beccaria's observations. I remember a lad of twenty, to whom I spoke for some time in his prison cell; he was thin, and had the lacklustre eyes of one who has given up hope. He had been tortured in a police station and had confessed to his theft. But the police had carried on; they possessed a large file of thefts for which the culprits had never been found, so they tortured him until, exhausted, he had finally 'confessed' to five other thefts with which he had had nothing to do. To put an end to his agony he had preferred to admit to crimes not his own: at least he would be sent to prison, and the torments would end.

Thus torture is more or less 'effective' according to the victim. Political prisoners and the more hardened criminals (especially certain dangerous drug traffickers) are more resistant to torments. The former have the strong support of an ideology: they are fighting for an ideal and have long known they might have to suffer for their political aims; they know other militant comrades have undergone the same tribulations and would feel humiliated if they were themselves unable to stand up to torture; sometimes they are afraid of reprisals, if they were to talk. The small beer and middle echelon drug peddlers are moved by other considerations: usually they are addicts, and sell drugs for motives other than mere profit; they are almost always habitual criminals, well used to being bullied by the police. For these and other categories of detainees, 'ordinary' torture is fairly useless: they do not confess. Thus, as I had occasion to note more than once, the police use more cruel and long-lasting techniques of torture on such criminals. States themselves facilitate these barbarous practices – probably unwittingly – because national laws often allow such categories of criminals to be held in custody for longer periods than other detainees (the usual justification for this is the need to prolong investigations to discover accomplices and collect compelling evidence).

Yet even with such hardened detainees, torture – as well as being repugnant to our conscience and degrading for both the victim and the torturer – reveals all the limitations Beccaria brought to our notice. I remember a long interview I had, in prison, with two young people, a man and a woman. They stood accused of belonging to a forbidden political organization, which the government suspected of using terrorist methods. They had both been subjected by the police to cruel forms of torture, which they described to us in detail and which our doctors found convincing and were borne out by their examinations. The man was about thirty, self-assured, with a well-kept beard, and spoke with calm and precision: he was obviously an experienced political leader with his head full of ideology and unshakeable convictions, and obviously certain he would be tortured again in future. He gave us a minute and detached description of what the police had done to him, adding that they had got nowhere: he had been determined not to speak, and had succeeded. He also said that when he had been taken before the public prosecutor before being transferred to prison, he had described the torture inflicted on him. The magistrate had shaken his head in disbelief, remarking: 'If they had tortured you, you would have talked!' The girl was just over twenty. She looked frail, with blue-black hair enhancing the extreme pallor of her face. Her hands trembled as she recalled the period of her detention. She had been arrested while distributing hand-outs for that political organization. She was obviously only a 'groupie'. She spoke with difficulty and told us, without any shame, that after the first electric shock (I will not give you the horrible details of how this had been administered) she had immediately admitted to everything imputed to her, to the point of inventing names and circumstances. As she spoke, I kept an eye on the young man: he remained impassive, without showing any solidarity or reproach.

This episode, to my mind, confirmed that the worst forms of torture – those practised against persons suspected of very serious crimes – are hardly ever 'effective' against those who may be 'guilty' but are strong-minded, yet can break the resistance of weaker people and make them 'confess', even to offences they never committed. All this is well known. To quote the forceful imagery of Beccaria once more: 'As punishments become more cruel, the minds of men, as a fluid rises to the same height as any object surrounding it, grow hardened and insensible.' Besides, the same was true in the past, when torture was far more horrendous and, above all, legally admitted as proof of guilt or innocence. The records of Tommaso Campanella's trial vividly recall the torture he was subjected to on 4 and 5 June 1601, in Naples, by an ecclesiastical court investigating his 'crime' of heresy. Since the Italian philosopher was pretending to be mad, the court first tried the 'rope' torture (the victim was suspended by a rope and kept there even after his arms had been wrenched from their sockets), then decided to try the 'vigil' on him. This consisted in a combination of two forms: the 'rope' and the 'trestle' (when the victim fainted while hanging suspended, he was made to sit on a sharp wooden trestle, which cut into the flesh of his thighs); the 'vigil' went on for forty consecutive hours. Such terrible and protracted suffering, combined with lack of sleep, made even the most obdurate suspects speak. Yet Campanella, who was tortured for thirty-six hours, with three brief interludes, continued to feign madness and would not admit to anything. At the end of these harrowing torments, all lacerated and bloody, he was taken by one of the jailers – who had to carry him in his arms, so weak was the philosopher – to an adjacent room, to be taken off to prison. According to a deposition (made on

20 July 1601) by that jailer, Campanella then said: 'Did they think me a fucking dolt, that I would talk?'

Though they may not possess Campanella's moral strength, many suspects manage to withstand our present-day tortures.

How we ascertained the existence of torture

The reader of these pages may by now be wondering how we managed, in many cases, to prove that the police do use such barbarous methods in certain European states.

Naturally, as I said before, we never caught a policeman ill-treating a victim. It would be naive to think such a thing possible: modern techniques of torture allow innocent-looking instruments to be hidden in a flash. This makes it is almost impossible for a group of foreign inspectors to enter a police station so suddenly as to catch the officers at their 'work'. The police are informed of the period of our visits, and, in the few countries where they brutalize suspects, they stop any violent ill-treatment for two or three weeks. They are also able to follow our movements from city to city with ease, and can thus predict our possible inspections. More than once we realized, even when we reached a police station unexpectedly, at the most unholy hours, that in a matter of minutes all the officers in that police station, as well as all those in the vicinity, knew of our arrival. On more than one occasion we were even followed by a police car, which could easily signal via radio our whereabouts and movements. (Once, I took some policemen by surprise as they waited for us outside our hotel, and told them we knew they were following us everywhere; they were terribly embarrassed and assured us it was for our protection, not for any other motive!)

If, then, it is absurd to expect to catch policemen

red-handed, how were we able to find that in certain countries torture *was practised*?

Non-governmental organizations proved valuable sources of information, especially Amnesty International and the group set up by Jean-Jacques Gautier, which I mentioned in chapter 1 and which is now called the Association for the Prevention of Torture; there were others, too, such as Helsinki Watch. These groups were often able to give us detailed reports, containing the names of the victims, where they were held prisoner, the kind of torture they had been subjected to, and so on. The information in these allegations is presumably collected from letters or the testimonies of relatives or reports of the victims' lawyers; sometimes the information is based on accounts given by the victims themselves, after they have been released. Though such information is useful, we have treated it with caution, either because we had no way of checking the original sources ourselves, or because they may have a fatal flaw: often they refer to political prisoners only; hence, they might contain an ideological or political slant, and in any case they do not give us any insight into another category of detainees, about whose welfare we care just as much, that is common criminals.

A second, more reliable, source is the direct testimony of the victims. To discover these, we did not content ourselves with looking for those whose names and places of detention had been given us by second-hand sources: we wanted to carry out our own inquiry, as impartially as possible. After our initial inspections we realized that it was futile to seek these persons in police stations: if a person had been brutalized before we arrived and still bore the resultant physical marks, that person could rapidly be transferred elsewhere (to another police station, far from there, or to a prison), or even be released. Naturally, we always scrutinized the custody records; whenever the sudden transferral or release of a detainee, a couple of days before our arrival – sometimes a matter of a few hours earlier – seemed suspect, we asked for precise information on the reasons for these movements and the exact destination of that person. We soon discovered how easy it was for the police to hoodwink us, giving us vague indications, sending us off to talk to other officials, or promising information which was never given. Only in a very few cases were we able to follow the track of detainees who had suddenly been transferred. Usually, after exhaustive research, we found them in a prison, and there we were able to interview them.

After these initial inspections we developed our own technique. On arriving at a prison, one group would go straight to the unit where newly arrived prisoners are received. Here we would interview all detainees on the conditions of the police stations they had just left, and one or two of our own doctors would examine them with great care. These new arrivals have often turned out to be veritable mines of misery: the doctors have frequently discovered signs of recent torture or serious ill-treatment. Meanwhile, another group of inspectors would take a careful look at the custody registers, select a sample of fifteen to twenty prisoners who had come in during the last two or three weeks: on discovering where they were held, these prisoners were interrogated and, if necessary, examined by one or more doctors.

We found that five types of evidence were of crucial importance: the testimony of the victims of torture; our doctors' examinations; the medical records compiled, at various times (for instance, before the detainee was transferred from a police station to a prison), by the medical officers of the country being visited; our discovery of places of torture – and during some lucky well-timed visits, the instruments themselves; and the reaction of police officers to all our precise and searching questions on the subject.

It does not take much to discern the difference between a truthful statement and one packed with lies and inventions. First, the prisoners we talk to know they have nothing to gain by lying to us; we warn them at once, before the interview, that we are not interested in knowing whether they are innocent or guilty, that we can do nothing to help them individually, because the reason for our inspection is only to discover the prevailing conditions of detention. Only political prisoners have any interest in inflating or exaggerating the ill-treatment they may have received. This we know, and so we always play down the evidence in such cases; besides, the questions we ask them are even more precise and meticulous, so as to discover contradictions or inexact information.

Of course, we always bear in mind the warnings which police officers have given us, in many countries, against the fantasies of detainees. The police feel that one must not forget that it is to the detainees' advantage to say that they have been seriously ill-treated, because they hope the judges will give them a lesser sentence; otherwise, when they come before the judges, they claim they have been tortured to retract any admission of guilt or other compromising testimony they may have given to the police; in some countries, where the 'turncoat' (a person who has turned Queen's evidence) receives a reduced sentence in exchange for telling the police the names and facts behind crimes, such people will later protect themselves from their mates in prison by saying that they had been forced to speak under torture.

On the whole it is not easy to determine how plausible an account of torture is. Decisive factors are: the details that prisoners can give on the method their tormentors adopted; the accuracy of the account of their mental and physical reactions; whether they can give a description of the premises where they were ill-treated and specifically indicate the equipment in the room where they were subjected to torture. The degree of precision of these accounts, together with the prisoners' attitude while they recount their experience (facial expression, body language, and other particulars that will not escape the careful observer), may all contribute to an impression of veracity, or may reveal instead that the description is based on the experiences of others, or even on the fantasies of a lively imagination. Another valid test of truthfulness may lie in the concordance of separate accounts given by various inmates of the same prison, the same town and the same country. By and large, policemen are not possessed with much imagination: they tend to use the same methods on all detainees; and the same techniques are used by their colleagues in other towns or villages of that state. This is why we always felt it was essential to collect a large number of testimonies, from a number of diverse victims, in different towns, especially when these persons were not accused of the same crimes (in a spectrum that went from terrorism to the various forms of common crime). The volume of these testimonies and the details they may contain constitute compelling indicators, if not conclusive proof, of torture. This approach was confirmed when, in the case of one country, we were able to establish that the numerous claims of 'political prisoners' to have been tortured, which – it is worth noting – were all made by people of the same persuasion, were highly suspect. In this case all the accounts were stereotyped, and the prisoners were unable to furnish us with convincing details and particulars such as to give each story its 'individual' character.

.   Naturally, each time we collected circumstantial evidence, we always tried to corroborate it by getting our doctors to make a careful examination of the victim. As a rule we subjected testimonies to minute and rigorous inquiry to ascertain their truthfulness. In many cases in which we were persuaded of this veracity, our doctors could find no physical trace of torture: this is quite normal, since, as I have already said, police officers know how to inflict torments that leave no marks. In many other cases, however, either because policemen had committed a mistake or because they had gone too far, or because too little time had elapsed after the torture, our doctors found traces that concurred with the detainees' allegations. To be one hundred per cent certain that we had reached the right conclusions, every time one of our doctors stated that traces and symptoms that corroborated the prisoner's statement had been found, I called in at least one other doctor from our delegation (often two) to make a separate examination, and accepted the findings of the former only if the others agreed with it.

What were these marks? Since I often assisted my medical colleagues (in that I took notes to their dictation while they carried out the examination), I can give an account of some of these cases. Frequently, our medical experts found evident sequelae of *fàlaka*, the technique I described earlier. Normally, in individuals who did not take much care of their skins, the soles of the feet were both swollen and smooth (due to the creams that had been applied to reduce the swelling). The palms of the hands often presented the same symptoms. In other cases the prisoners had bruises on certain parts of their bodies (the back, the legs or the chest, for example), which bore out their claims to have been repeatedly beaten with a truncheon or a thick rubber tube. In other cases our doctors confirmed that the shoulder-blade area was swollen, which they felt could only be the result of a prolonged unnatural position (the detainees had had their hands tied behind their backs and had been hung for some time from a rope attached to a hook: this painful and abnormal position had slightly dislocated the humeral bones and provoked a faint swelling that could be discovered by careful and expert palpation). In other cases our colleagues found burns on parts of the body where they would never be self-inflicted, either on purpose or unintentionally (such as tiny burns on the penis). Other examples – of a more gruesome nature – are detailed in an official document (the Public Statement on Turkey, adopted by our Committee on 15 December 1992), and I would rather refer you to that than describe them here.

We also gave not a little credit to certificates issued by the medical officers of the countries we visited: these came from police or prison medical officers, or from private doctors whose visit had been requested by the detainee. In numerous cases these certificates confirmed the statements of the detainees and were used by our medical experts either to corroborate their own findings, or – in cases of persons tortured long before our visit, and on whom our doctors had not been able to find any tell-tale traces – as supporting evidence of the victims' claims. Often our medical experts visited state departments of forensic medicine, to observe how the examination of detainees was carried out, before their transfer to prison; or to check their medical files. On several occasions, they asked to see the autopsy reports for persons suspected of having died after being severely tortured: these reports frequently confirmed our suspicions.

Needless to say, and without much hope of success, we always searched for the places and instruments of torture. For reasons I have already given, we were hardly ever successful. Yet in some specific cases, we managed to put our hands on something tangible.

For instance, in one country, the central police station in a small town had earned a very bad reputation. Hence, we decided not only to inspect the premises with all due care, but also to search all the main prisons in the town for persons who had recently spent one or more days in police custody there. After exhausting inquiries, we were able to meet a dozen prisoners. Most of them had been gravely ill-treated. Three or four, in particular, had been hooded, tied by the feet and hung from a hook in the ceiling: as they dangled, head down, they had been beaten on the back and chest with a flexible stick (possibly a truncheon). Our medical examination revealed nothing: there were signs on their bodies, but our doctors felt they did not prove anything, since they could have been caused by fights, scuffles at the moment of arrest, or even self-inflicted. However, the prisoners gave us such precise accounts that we were puzzled. The information each of them gave us tallied surprisingly; it should be noted that these people had never been held together, either at the police station, or in prison, so they had not been able to concoct a common version of the facts. We collected all the data, and I asked for sketches of the premises where they had been tortured. One element seemed particularly important to me: despite the blindfold or hood over their eyes, they had seen – either under the hood, or after it had been taken off – the hook in the ceiling through which a rope was passed to hoist them up by the feet. With the help of all these details and the sketches, we returned to the police station for a second visit and concentrated on three offices on the second floor, where the prisoners claimed to have been tortured. In each of these offices we did find a large metal hook screwed into the ceiling near a door, which tallied exactly with the descriptions we had been given. I asked several officers why the hooks were to be found in those rooms, and not elsewhere, and what they were used for. The answers varied greatly: some policemen said they had never noticed them, and did not know what purpose they served; others said the hooks had been there, already, when the police took over the building as their headquarters ten years previously; others suggested they might have been used to hang large fans (an absurd explanation since the hook was ten centimetres away from the door, leaving no room for the blades of a

fan). The obvious embarrassment of the police officers
and the implausible nature of their explanations reassured
us that we had found what we were looking for.

We came to similar conclusions in another country.
Here, too, we were visiting police stations without previous warning, though this time we had heard no claims
of ill-treatment. In the station, located in a very crowded
district – we had turned up unexpectedly, though perhaps
the news had been buzzed through by walkie-talkie – the
police officers received us courteously, took us round their
offices, the interrogation rooms and two cells. We asked if
there were other cells, but they said we had seen everything. We inspected many rooms, on three floors, and
were about to leave, feeling rather puzzled because something did not tally. Near the entrance to the station, one
of our colleagues left the group and started to wander
aimlessly around the building, moving fairly fast, tailed by
a policeman. Then, having discovered a somewhat hidden
stair that led downwards, he called us all to join him. We
rushed away from the group of officers we were talking to,
descended three flights, and found a set of offices connected to an area divided into two sections: one was taken
up by a cell fifteen metres square, the other subdivided
into tiny cells.

While my colleagues, followed by a posse of policemen,
inspected these two sections and then – having demanded
to be left alone – interviewed the detainees, I started to go
over the offices one by one, in the area preceding the
detention cells. The police, though visibly irritated, did
nothing to stop me. After a while I found a locked door,
had it opened, and found a small whitewashed room with
no furniture – unlike the other offices in that basement –
except for two broken chairs. What surprised me most,
however, were two projectors, hanging from the ceiling, at
about a metre from one of the walls, pointing towards it. I
asked what the room was used for; they said it was used

for the recognition of criminals by eye witnesses; indeed, they drew my attention to a one-way mirror in the door (by turning on the lights in the room, and turning off those outside, one could see in and not be seen). I tried to turn on the projectors: one had its lamp missing, and the other did not work. How could they use the room, if the lights did not work? I got no answer. I went on with my inspection, found numerous traces of blood along the wall on which the projectors faced; I also found two large metal hooks, of about fifty centimetres each in diameter, screwed into the middle of the ceiling. I asked about the blood and the large hooks, but was given evasive and contradictory answers: some said those hooks had always been there, and were not used; others merely shrugged. When I pointed out that it was odd those hooks should exist only in that one room, and nowhere else in the basement or in the offices on the other floors, I again got no reply. As to the blood, some said they had no idea why it was there, others that some 'criminals' taken to the room might have done themselves an injury, especially since many were drug addicts.

The ill-concealed irritation of the police, their absurd answers, the position of the little room (close to the cells, in a segregated area of the station), the absence of furniture, together with the two large hooks and the blood stains on the wall, convinced me and my colleagues that this was a place in which detainees were probably tortured. Naturally, my colleagues went back to question the inmates in the cells, doing so with great caution. But although they admitted to having been violently ill-treated more than once, they said they had never been taken to the room we had just seen, and naturally we were unable to discover whether they were telling us the truth or were afraid of being subjected to reprisals later.

In two other cases, however, we were absolutely certain of our deductions, also because we acted on precise indications given to us by detainees in several prisons. In the jail of a large town in one of the countries we visited, a considerable number of common criminals had told us they had received electric shocks on the tenth floor of the police headquarters. Their crimes varied from theft to robbery with violence and drug trafficking. They had all received the same treatment, before and after their interrogations. We were so struck by the similar behaviour of the police in all these cases that we asked for a detailed description of the premises where they had been allegedly tortured. They all said they had been tied to a small bed, and had then had electrodes applied to their gums or genitals. After each application they had been taken to sit on a row of chairs nearby, where other detainees were awaiting their turn. The new victim was then tied to the bed and subjected to electric shocks, while the others were forced to listen to the shrieks. Armed with rudimentary sketches of the building, a group of our inspectors went to the police station and asked to see the eighth floor. At the end of their visit, pretending to go towards the exit, they suddenly ran for all their worth up to the tenth floor, with their police escort unable to stop them. When they reached the room that had been described, they found a detainee handcuffed to a radiator, in the dark, obviously awaiting his turn to be interrogated. They saw at once that the room had been divided by a thin partition, obviously erected very recently, behind which was hidden a small metal-spring bed, upholstered in foam rubber with a plastic covering; to each side of the bed were attached four canvas straps. At one end, and in the centre, the plastic covering had worn through and the foam rubber had been burnt. On the wall beside the bed were four electric plugs, recently plastered over. The police officers answered our questions with some embarrassment: the plugs had been used for a telephone, to light a red lamp outside the door, for the aerial of a radio. They added that both the partition and the plastering of the plugs had been effected in the last two days (we had arrived in that town two days earlier), without being able to explain why this work had been carried out. We also noticed a row of four chairs, against one wall in the room. Naturally, the way the furniture and other details dovetailed perfectly with the descriptions we had received, together with the ridiculous explanations given us by the police, left us in no doubt as to what went on in that room.

We had a similar experience in a city in another European country. Several prisoners, held for common crimes, had described in detail a room on the top floor of the central police station. There they had been tied to a beam, arms spread horizontally as on a cross, and hoisted mid-air; they had then been tortured with truncheon blows and electric shocks to various parts of the body. Although they had always been blindfolded, some of them had managed to see minute details. One had seen, in a flash, something written on the door into the room. Another gave us a precise description of the material used to blindfold his eyes. Another said he thought the 'cross' must have hung from a hook in the middle of the room, because when he had been given the electric shocks his legs had swung violently to and fro without touching anything; thus, he could not have been hung against a wall. Yet another told us that he had been kept naked during the various 'sessions', but between each he had been made to wear a pair of dungarees, and remembered the exact colour.

With all these details in mind, we again managed to disconcert the police, who were unable to keep up with us as we ran up to the top floor. We found the room, with all its equipment and the other implements listed by the detainees. However, the large wooden bar, to which the victims were tied and hoisted, was not attached to two hooks in the ceiling – as we had imagined – but straddled two metal cupboards, full of paper and other heavy objects, which acted as supports. I well remember the dismay and embarrassment of the chief officer, who rushed upstairs, as well as that of his collaborators, as they stood there watching us make a detailed inventory of these items. His embarrassment was so acute he started to give explanations that made even his officers smile. In two offices opposite we found some small first-aid cupboards, containing the anti-inflammatory creams the detainees had described, as well as a truncheon, carefully hidden away. Let me add that the three rooms, with a kind of toilet annex, were hermetically sealed off from the rest of the offices and cells on that floor.

After taking our leave of the police, I felt it would be useful to make one last crucial test. For this reason, seven or eight hours later, I went back to the police station (it was late at night) to visit the cells in the basement. After inspecting these for a couple of hours, I asked to speak to the head officer in his office. He received us very civilly. I begged him to do me a special favour: as our group now included a particularly important member, who had not been with us that morning, could he possibly show us the room and the offices we had discovered then? He agreed, but explained that that morning he himself had been unpleasantly surprised to find things in that room 'that should not have been there'; he had not known of their existence, because he was always so busy and did not have the time to look into every room in the building; after we had left he had given immediate orders to have those 'instruments' removed; if we went up, there would be none of the things we had seen in the morning. And so it was; only the two metal cupboards remained in the room. Of course, his tardy explanation was for us the equivalent of a full confession.

Similar discoveries were made in another country we visited. We had been told by various detainees, held both in prison and in police stations, that in a certain town people suspected of serious crimes, especially drug trafficking or armed robbery, were repeatedly beaten by the police with wooden sticks on various parts of the body. One day we descended on the main police station, the one mentioned in all the accusations. Instead of following our usual routine (a talk with the chief inspector, a visit to all the cells and, last, a visit to the offices), we split into two groups and went straight up to the floors occupied by the offices of the two risky squads: narcotics and armed robbery. On each of these floors, while one of us engaged the duty officer in talk, the others undertook a rapid inspection of the various rooms. We came across a large number of sticks – some made of wood, some metal – hidden away behind the officers' desks and in the interrogation rooms. The embarrassment of the police was acute when we asked what those sticks and cudgels were used for: their explanations varied greatly and were all implausible, if not ridiculous. In any case, when we went back, two days later, the entire arsenal had disappeared, and the reasons given for their removal were as absurd as the ones given two days earlier.

A more dramatic episode occurred when we managed to find a stick for giving electric shocks in a police station in yet another European country. Various prisoners, all of them jailed for drug trafficking, had told us that in a certain police station they had been badly ill-treated, and had in particular been given electric shocks. Some, since they had not been blindfolded during this electric shock treatment, gave us a careful description of the official who usually administered that form of torture and of the other man who gave the orders, sitting behind his desk. They also described the little dark stick, made of plastic and battery run, from which two sharp needles emerged, and which the torturer had applied to very delicate parts of the body. No traces remained of these electric shocks, but the

86

descriptions were so detailed, and so congruent (even though the prisoners had no means of communicating), that we felt we must visit these premises.

Our visit evoked no surprise; we had already been in town for several days, and obviously all the police stations had been alerted. What did amaze them – a fact that soon became obvious – was the meticulousness of our inspection. After hours of questions and interviews with the police, we began to have the cupboards and drawers opened in each office in the narcotics section. Often the keys to the doors or the locks of the cupboards could not be found – we wondered why. In spite of our great concern for the damage we were causing, which we offered to pay for, we had the police officers force those doors and locks, and we went through everything with great care. However, when we came to a metal cupboard closed with two padlocks, in one officer's room, we were met with a firm refusal: they would not allow us to open it. Why? The officer in question was on leave. I was talking to the chief inspector, an insignificant little man who looked rather frightened (his subordinates interrupted him continually, answering in his stead and showing a complete lack of respect). He said, hesitantly, that he did not have the keys to the two locks, nor could he order it to be forced open, without the policeman being present. I countered that the man must be found at once, since he was known to be in town. In any case, if he was not found, we would open the cupboard, without looking closely at his personal effects. Since the cupboard was in an office in which the man worked and, in particular, where he interrogated persons held in custody, we had a right to inspect its contents. At this stage the chief inspector – who had been drawn aside by two officers for a hurried and excited confabulation – produced a new theory to justify his refusal: had anything been missing after our inspection, the said policeman could have made an official protest. I tried not to lose my temper and asked if a search conducted by international inspectors in front of police officers could possibly raise any suspicion of theft. The police inspector looked more and more tense and unsure of his ground. He changed his line and remarked that we might find that things were missing from that cupboard that should have been there, and the officer could have complained of this later. We answered that this argument was very flimsy indeed. My suspicions were growing, confirmed by various factors: the chief inspector's stubbornness and perplexity, his nebulous objections, the furtive confabulations that were being held among groups of worried policemen, frequent invitations to go for a cup of coffee or tea, in the director's office (an obvious and naive attempt to get us out of the office, over which we had been presiding for some hours). When I finally put the inspector on the spot, saying that I would have to make a detailed report on his refusal, he looked almost relieved: he asked me to do so and to note that it had been impossible to check the contents of the cupboard. He thought he could beat me in stubbornness, but this was not to be. I sat down and slowly wrote out my report. Then I asked to telephone a high-ranking official in the Ministry of the Interior, who had given us his number on the first day of our visit, a routine procedure for our delegations (we use these numbers in emergencies). I ignored the man's protests – he was looking ever more tired and resigned – and his attempts to dissuade me. At last I spoke to the high-ranking official (I had gone to the chief inspector's office, but I had left two colleagues to keep an eye on the cupboard). After listening patiently to my brief account of what had happened, the ministerial official asked to speak to the chief inspector and gave orders to do as I asked.

A policeman took a crowbar and, after a few minutes' effort, forced the cupboard door open. All of a sudden the office filled with policemen; they all crowded round the tables and along the walls, watching our every movement as we scrutinized the contents of the cupboard. This was chock full of paper and other objects. We proceeded to take an inventory, piece by piece, of all those objects. One of us took each item and put it on a table, another wrote a description of the nature and appearance of the object, a third kept an eye on the whole scene. Clearly, as we went ahead, the tension among the policemen was rising: they kept on whispering excitedly. At one stage I had to ask some of them to leave the room, since there was no air left. After about twenty minutes (our inspection was proceeding very slowly and carefully), the colleague who was taking the objects from the cupboard removed a short plastic stick, round and black, with a button on the handle and two metal needles at the other end. As soon as he placed it on the table, I seized it and pressed the button: an electric shock passed between the needles: a short bluish flash. It was frightening enough just to see it. When I put it back on the table, I noticed the police had all disappeared: we were now alone with the chief inspector (later on, a colleague who joined us a few seconds after our discovery told me he had heard one of the policemen say, as he left the room, 'They've found it!'). I asked the chief inspector what the black stick was used for. He said he did not know: obviously it was a personal belonging of the officer who owned the cupboard.

As if by magic, that same policeman telephoned us ten minutes later, to ask if he could meet us. We accepted promptly. He looked almost exactly like the description we had been given by some of the prisoners. About thirty-five, short and thick-set, with an air of great agility. He had an ordinary, inexpressive face: the only notable feature, apart from a little black moustache, was his sly rather than intelligent expression. I shivered; here before me for the first time since the beginning of our inspections was a man who was undoubtedly a torturer. The man was very tense during our interview, but he kept his self-control. He assured us the stick was for his own personal defence, especially against the dogs that drug traffickers use so often. I asked him if it was legal in that country for a policeman to carry an electric stick, since he obviously went around armed with a pistol (I had noticed one in his belt, behind his back, when he had taken off his jacket). With a tight-lipped look, he admitted it was illegal, but added that the narcotics squad met with such danger that he had felt it necessary to break the rule. He appeared to be reciting a part, having been hurriedly briefed on what to say to justify his possession of that instrument. He even tried to improvise a brief explanation when I asked him why he kept the stick in the office where he interrogated suspects. But I felt certain he himself was not sure of what he was saying, and above all that he knew we did not believe him.

None of us revealed the disgust or contempt we felt for the torturer. We had to keep our feelings to ourselves. We thus made an effort to be content with having, finally, got our hands on one of the most modern and widespread implements of torture. As I went dejectedly back to the hotel, I remembered something Henri Bergson is supposed to have said before he died in his beloved Paris when, in 1940, it had been occupied by the Nazis: 'We can count ourselves fortunate for having seen, with our own eyes, prehistoric man.' (For the reader curious to know what happened next, let me add that, a few days later, during our last meeting with the state authorities, we described what we had found – though the Minister of the Interior had obviously been informed – and asked for immediate inquiries and the incrimination of the guilty parties; the authorities promptly did as we asked, but applied only disciplinary sanctions. Obviously, the Committee must return to that country to find out if only one or two persons were punished, or whether there has been a radical change in the practice of police interrogations.)

7

Common Criminals and Terrorists

In September 1993 I resigned from the Committee: I could no longer absorb all that suffering and degradation witnessed during our inspections. It was to be expected: take any lawyer with an average resistance to physical and mental pain, tear him away from his tranquil and recondite studies, throw him into places where reality is harsh and distressing; in a little while his resistance will break down. The inspections conducted by the Strasbourg Committee are very tiring, not only because of the massive doses of anguish and affliction we perceived on the faces of many detainees. Our movements within the country we were visiting were often very uncomfortable: they took place at unnatural hours, by train, plane or taxi, as we always refused the offer of official limousines and escort. The visits are interspersed with agitated meetings among inspectors in dingy rooms, or in the corridors and entrance halls of hotels. They also involve rapid exchanges of information or ideas over breakfast, lunch or dinner; close study of penal codes and penitentiary regulations; constant consultation of notes taken before leaving, as it is necessary to have accurate documentation on the country we are visiting; finally, the short, desolate prison meals, sparse and spartan food supplied by the authorities (which we always insist on paying for, even when it is frankly inedible). We also suffer from the frustration of not being able to see what is beautiful in that country, since all our efforts are concentrated on carrying through the job as scrupulously and effectively as possible.

Now that I have parted from my inspector colleagues, when insomnia is most persistent my mind is invaded not only by the places we visited, carefully enclosed spaces set aside for pain, but also by the innumerable faces of people I met. To shake off these ghosts, I sometimes talk about them to a close friend or two; sometimes I have compared myself, ironically, to Ulysses (remembering how the shades of the dead surface out of the Erebus and assail him, crowding round him, trying to touch and talk to him – after he had dug a trench a cubit wide and made sacrifices to evoke Tiresias and ask about his own future – and Ulysses, pale with fear, keeps the shades at bay by brandishing his sword). I, too, keep my shades at a distance somehow, by speaking of them to my best friends, and now by conjuring them up for you, as best I can.

The limits and aims of our work did not give us room for more than a few hours' contact with the prisoners we met. Indeed, as I have already said, one of our basic rules was to tell them at once why we were there: that we could not follow up single cases, and hence did not want to know if they were guilty or innocent, and that we could do nothing for them as individuals. We were there to examine the conditions of detention, to see if prisoners had been subjected to ill-treatment or violence, and to prevent possible abuse. In the beginning, I thought such a premise would put them off: they would refuse to speak to us, or hardly deign to pay us any attention. Instead, we always found people who were not only prepared to talk to us but seemed eager to do so. Occasionally, after a day spent in a prison, word would get round via the prison grape-vine, and we would be besieged with requests for interviews and would then have to make a selection. Perhaps prisoners are avid to talk to someone who is not attached to the penitentiary system: one who is neither a cell mate nor the representative of the state apparatus. There is a real desire to tell their stories – perhaps to make a clean breast of it – to people prepared to listen attentively, though dispassionately.

In all these years I met with only two refusals: once in Spain, where two ETA prisoners got a companion to tell me that they would not speak to us, without giving any explanation. Another time, in France, we were going round the rather depressing disciplinary unit of a large prison; I asked to speak to a foreigner who had been there for a long time, and of whom I knew only that he had asked repeatedly, in vain, to serve his prison term in his own country; he was about to be released. The door was opened and we saw a sort of human larva lying on the bed, the sheet pulled up to his chin: he yelled at us, cursing and swearing, that we had come too late; we could go to hell.

At other times we were able to overcome initial hostility. I remember meeting with a woman who was suspected of terrorist attacks and was therefore being held in a female prison in a large European country. Though she was still quite young, her body was matronly and had gone to seed; her face was intelligent, with regular features, but had lost its freshness. She had been brought into that prison a few hours before we met. Unlike the other detainees, she greeted us coldly, asking numerous questions about our duties and job. I got the feeling she suspected that we were in league with the authorities and that our interview was meant to throw new light on the details of her life. She answered very laconically, giving us very few details about her stay in the police station; but she did not object to our coming back the next day. A few hours later, the deputy governor – a man well-thought of by the women prisoners

for the humanity and understanding he showed – told me
that before meeting us, the lady had been very hostile, not
only to the prison warders, but to the other prisoners who
had tried to approach her and help her. The next day,
when we reached her unit, two other prisoners told us at
once that the woman had behaved less suspiciously, after
meeting us, and had started to talk to them; she had also
asked to see us. When we met her she was transformed.
Spontaneously she set about telling us of her arrest, her
previous life, of how the police had treated her. What was
the key to such a change? The previous day my colleague,
with great simplicity, had known how to deal with the
woman's hostile reserve, woman to woman, showing her
great respect and comprehension. Slowly the prisoner had
realized that she could trust us.

Other cases, in which detainees seemed very reluctant
to talk, struck us as being more justified. For instance, in
a large police station where there were many people
suspected of political offences, especially terrorism, we
asked to see a middle-aged man, who had been held for
almost a week. He looked very run-down, fattish and
unwell. He gave us a frightened look and said at once he
had nothing to say. But he did not walk out (we had
decided to speak to the detainees in a room of our own
choice, to avoid the possibility of eavesdroppers). One of
my medical colleagues, a man of long experience and with
a very humane manner, asked him a few more questions,
gently and without insisting. After a little the man said he
had eight children. He stopped, and then repeated the
same phrase two or three times. At this point the doctor
took his hands (he was sitting opposite) and told him we
respected him, that he did not have to talk: it was not
necessary. The man thanked him with a nod, got up and
made for the door; then he stopped, and instead of going
out, he turned towards us and, without uttering a word,
pulled up the thick jersey and the shirt he had on, and

showed us his torso with huge black and blue bruises in diagonal stripes. The doctor nodded. The man pulled down his clothes and went out.

In the police station of another country, we met a young man suspected of terrorism. It was night time, and we decided to interview him in an office quite near his cell (only later did we realize that this was the room used for interrogations, full of hidden microphones and a video camera, also out of sight, which the police used to observe the detainees while they were being questioned). He was a fine-looking young man, who said little: a few details on his job before he had been arrested, adding that he had nothing to complain about. I looked at his unshaven pointed face, his red eyes, his miserable clothes: the young man was so full of suffering I asked my colleagues to interrupt the interview. The detainee's face was a blank as he was led back to his cell. Two days later, when we had discovered that we had been using one of the interrogation rooms, and that the man had known this, we went back to see him. This time we entered his cell and preferred not to ask any questions; one of our doctors asked if he would like to be visited. He refused. The doctor took his leave with a handshake. I went up, hand outstretched: he had obviously recognized me and took my hand in both of his, looking me straight in the eye.

You may well ask whether I believed every word I was told by the detainees. The answer, of course, is no. But it was not difficult, after a while, to notice when they were embroidering or telling lies. In any case, as far as possible, we always checked what we had been told. However, I usually had the impression that the detainees we interviewed were, on the whole, telling us the truth (all the more so since they had nothing to gain from telling lies). To a certain extent this was possible because we always chose to interview them far from the eyes of the police and warders, or at least where we could not be overheard.

Sometimes the prison governor, feeling responsible for our safety, would ask us to leave the cell door ajar, telling a prison officer to stand nearby, in case we needed help. We always accepted such precautions, so long as we were allowed to talk without being overheard.

On other occasions we found ourselves in quite risky situations, but nothing dramatic ever occurred. I well remember one instance, in the high-security section of a large prison, when we asked to speak freely to the only detainee, a man with a life sentence for having committed many murders, some while already in jail. The warder let us into the cell, leaving the door open and adding that we could walk up and down the corridor which led to his guard room. We spoke to the detainee at length; he was a strapping, thick-set young man, with a nervy smile and a wild look in his eye; he gave us a very detailed description of conditions there. After a little, when we went into the corridor to stretch our legs, I realized that the guard had disappeared and closed the heavy gate that separated this section from the others. Meanwhile, the prisoner, feeling rather excited at having spoken to three people – having been alone for so long – began to tell us about his latest exploit: a few months earlier he had knifed and killed another prisoner, sentenced for having molested little children; he added that he could now take the law into his own hands in prison, as he had nothing to lose, and a few years back he had even taken some people hostage to organize his escape. I began to feel rather tense. Fortunately, there was a psychiatrist among us: he noticed I was showing my nerves, and became more cordial with the prisoner, patting him on the back. It all ended well; the prisoner even helped us to call the missing guard to shut him up again and let us out of that section. As we were moving off, he smiled and said he would never have harmed us, as he found us 'likeable'.

I often wondered why we should be considered 'likeable'. I think the answer is that we always considered and treated detainees, even those who had committed horrendous crimes, as people who were being held in a state of mental and bodily constriction – not only because they had been shut away, but frequently because the conditions of detention were so bad; in short, we tried never to forget that these were people who were suffering. The detainees probably felt that we looked at them with different eyes: different from those of the prison officers, but also from those of social workers, prison doctors and psychologists or the chaplain, that is, different from those of officials whose job it was to help them individually to solve concrete issues. Perhaps they were struck by the fact that we did not ask them about the nature of their crime, the length of their sentence, or whether they were guilty or innocent. I must confess that, besides my understanding for their current circumstances, I often felt no horror for their crimes, even when I knew them to be extremely serious. Those detainees were people whose past, for the purposes of our job, meant little to us. For instance, I remember talking to a robber and murderer, famous for escaping in a helicopter from the prison where he was being held for his first set of crimes. After a long flight, he had been captured by the police in a neighbouring state, following a bloody gun battle. I had read about his exploits in the newspapers, and when I reached the prison where he was held in the high-security section, I discovered he was respected and held in awe by everyone; even the guard, who was taking me to his cell, told me in semi-admiring tones that a few days after being imprisoned there, he had already got hold of a map of the building. This star of crime did not look the muscular and menacing Rambo type; he had a slight stammer, was respectful and polite, and seemed to suffer from claustrophobia.

In another country I met a man accused of having raped several little girls. We knew he had been arrested in the early days of our inspection, but could not discover where he was being held. Evidently the police were questioning him and did not want us to get in their way. Finally, after several visits to the same large police station, I was told he was in one of their security cells and that we could meet him. While we were waiting for the interview, of his own accord an inspector showed us the inquiring magistrate's report, with a list of the offences he was supposed to have committed. They were appalling. As I waited and waited, with a colleague and an interpreter, I began to tell them of my only other experience with someone accused of similar crimes, in a different European country: the rapist had been a nice-looking young black man with a broad smile; despite the smile he was, however, very tense, especially when he was talking to the woman who was interviewing him with me; when we left, my colleague confided in an exhausted voice that for the first time in our inspections she had felt waves of aggressiveness coming from the prisoner, an almost explosive danger, and she had been very frightened. It was silly to have told this story at that stage, because the interpreter – an attractive woman who usually showed great self-control – became scared and asked not to sit next to the detainee, as she usually did, but between the two of us. A look of relief crossed her face when the rapist entered the little room we had had to choose for our interview. He was under thirty, very short (not more than one and a half metres), thin, with a large belly and obtuse eyes. His sullen and aggressive expression contrasted strangely with that prematurely aged boy's body. Part of his face was swollen and, from time to time, he stopped talking and took great gulps of air (our doctor felt he probably had two broken ribs). The interview was held in a room connecting others, so we were often interrupted by police-men and detainees passing through. The man had decided not to let the authorities and his inmates know our doctor

was visiting him (he was afraid of reprisals); he would take
a quick sly look at the doors, whip up his clothes and show
us parts of his body. Despite the unpleasant look in his
eyes, almost without realizing it, we soon forgot the
terrible offences of which he stood accused and concentrated on the brutality with which he had been treated by
the police.

On several occasions we met detainees who, whatever
their crime, had an undeniable sense of dignity. I remember a transvestite we met in the prison of a very large
country. We had been given his name by a human rights
association, partly because his was an emblematic case,
but also because he had joined that association. He was
extremely young and good-looking; although he dressed
and behaved like a woman, he did so unostentatiously, or
at least with great naturalness. He stated at once that he
was very well treated in prison. To protect him from being
the butt of other prisoners, the governor had put him in
the company of other transvestites, in a special unit where
they were safe and could organize their own community
life. The only problem, a little one at that, was that as
soon as they had entered the jail their hair had been cut,
as was the custom for all prisoners, and they had been
forced to keep it short. He then described the abuse he
had been subjected to in police stations, where he had not
only been taunted and, perhaps, robbed of all the money
he had, but had also been physically humiliated. He had
decided to combat the odious behaviour of the police
towards homosexuals and transvestites. There was no
point in making a formal plea before a judge – he claimed
– because there was no hope of obtaining redress in that
country for such cases (it was very difficult to produce
evidence, and also judges had very little sympathy for the
category to which he belonged). He had decided to
continue his battle at a political level, by joining the
human rights association and trying to inspire the other

transvestites with a social conscience, to make them understand that the discrimination they suffered was a mere fragment of the greater problems that country had to face.

In my meetings with detainees, one source of distress to me was the frustration I felt at not being able to do anything concrete to help them – often their very obvious sufferings could have been alleviated quite easily, with a small gesture of good will. We had set ourselves very rigid rules, based on three main considerations. First, as I have already said, the principal aim of our mission (to scrutinize general conditions of detention) forced us to avoid looking for and trying to solve single cases, except in occasional and highly dramatic instances. Second, we avoided talking to the authorities about specific cases for fear that they might take it out on those individuals 'guilty' of having made complaints and criticisms. Third, by telling detainees right from the start that we could not give their names to the police or prison officers, not even to suggest improvements in the conditions of specific cases, we could count on gaining their confidence and receiving testimonies that they might otherwise have kept to themselves.

The fact remains that any form of action, however modest, to alleviate the suffering of some detainees, was prevented by our own rigid rules. I cannot forget what happened in the juvenile section of a large prison. As we went on our rounds, we came upon a long, narrow and very cold cell, with a faint light piercing a barred window; here, sitting on the lower bunk bed, we found two sixteen-year-old lads. They looked dejected and frightened, their faces and hands covered in bruises. They had been jailed for minor thefts and had been bullied and ill-treated by other prisoners, though we were not told why. Hence they had decided to escape and had rather naively thought that this would be easy. After trying various routes, they had ended up in the guards' section, had hidden themselves and fallen asleep. When the guards found them, still asleep, they were beaten violently as a punishment for attempting to escape. They were now in the disciplinary section, lost and confused, awaiting who knows what other forms of punishment. They were both thin, miserably dressed and dirty, representing that social distress born of the lack of a caring environment, poor schooling and lack of work, which almost always produces prison fodder. The boys spoke in low voices and mangled phrases, telling us what had happened as if it were all quite normal, an inevitable part of their daily lives. Suddenly, one of them started to sob, and a little later the other followed suit. Our interpreter, forgetting her professional stance, felt unable to translate the convulsive sentences of one of the boys, who went on talking through his sobs. It was all too much for me, too, and I retired to a corner of the cell. Luckily, my colleague was a woman and went to sit between the boys, with her arms around their shoulders and held them in a motherly hug. The interpreter did not need to translate what she was saying: the tone of her voice was clearly filled with compassion. The lads calmed down, and we decided to ask no more questions. Later, we discussed at length whether we should say a few words to the prison governor, urging him to intervene, but decided reluctantly to stick to our rule and say nothing.

Only once did I decide to do something for a detainee – precious little in fact. This was nothing directly connected to her detention, hence our rules were not broken. In a female prison, we entered a cell where there was a black African girl. She was small, thin, her face the very picture of anxiety; she could not conceal her agitation. Her answers were monosyllabic: everything was all right, she had no complaints either about the police, at the time of her arrest, or about the prison authorities. She talked in such a convulsive way it was obvious she was keeping something back. We asked her what was the matter and she burst out with the truth: she was about to have an operation (to remove a cyst) that might leave her sterile. This meant life in death, once she got back to her own country, which was in a year's time: there any woman who could not bear children was despised as useless. She begged us to ask the prison governor to stop the operation, or ask the surgeons to make sure she remained fertile. I spoke to the governor, an amiable and well-disposed man. Luckily, he knew all about the case, shared our concern, understood the girl's predicament perfectly, and had already spoken to the doctors. The latter had made no promises: they had to take the risk. The governor said he would have another try, so we went back to the girl, to reassure her.

So far I have spoken only of common criminals. In many ways our experiences with terrorists were similar, but not always so. When, after a day spent talking to thieves, murderers or drug traffickers – usually rough and uneducated individuals – I talked to a terrorist, I almost felt, if not relief, at least a sharper interest. Most terrorists, in fact, are motivated by ideals and are interested in acquiring an education. Furthermore, they are usually more intelligent than other detainees. This made our interviews with them more intriguing, as well as more dangerous, because their ideological motives and their intellectual background cause them to give misleading and inaccurate information.

After many interviews with terrorists, of differing ideological persuasion and in different countries, I have noticed certain common characteristics. First, solidarity, so to speak: they try to form a compact group along ideological lines and keep apart from other detainees. Their reaction to life in prison is self-discipline, self-control, and they read their own 'classics'. More than once we were unable to talk to a terrorist without having first to listen to a long generic speech from the official spokesman and to obtain permission to do so. Usually, they affect a certain disdain for common criminals. In a Spanish prison, I remember hearing a terrorist explain that the other prisoners took drugs, made brutes of themselves, were dirty, tended to blame the prison authorities and the prison warders most of all for everything; by contrast, terrorists saw the state as their real enemy. More generally, terrorists despised other prisoners because they 'let themselves go', whereas they react by clinging to a group ethic, by self-discipline and by using their time to study.

And yet, their very rigidity made our interviews more difficult: they almost always tried to manipulate us, to use us as a political vehicle for their ideals and demands. We rarely met a terrorist who, quite unconsciously, could arouse the same degree of human sympathy we might feel for common criminals. Few of these come to mind. One was the detainee I mentioned in chapter 5: that gaunt, emaciated man, with a blue chin and lively, hollow eyes, I met in the anti-terrorist section of a police station, lying in the dark on his straw pallet. The man, who had clearly lost his sense of time, struck me for the sobriety of his answers, the lack of any complaint, as if his suffering were in the nature of things. He did not give us the impression of wanting to transmit any political message. His extreme poverty was easy to read on his face, his clothes, his manner. Suffering was obviously his daily bread, both within and without his prison cell, hence he neither protested nor complained. Each of our questions was followed by short, precise answers. When we left, he thanked us for having spoken to him, and smiled for the first time – a wan smile.

The other I remember was young; he had been sentenced to life imprisonment for having assassinated several policemen. He was thin and wiry, with a short beard and very black eyes. He received us with mundane courtesy, showing an instant interest in our being there and great pleasure in talking to us. He had already served eight years in solitary confinement, and knew he would spend his remaining life alone. He could take exercise twice a day, each time for an hour. He uttered no complaints. He merely remarked he was really sorry he could do no work: his life would have been transformed if he had been allowed to speak to other political prisoners; however – he added – he was lucky enough to have a radio, to be allowed books, and could speak frequently to another terrorist who was in a nearby cell by yelling through the window. He added that the governor had offered him a television set, but he had turned it down, 'as he did not want to become a barbarian'. We spent a long time with him, without an interpreter, because he had taught himself English and spoke it very well. We talked about the books he was reading, all of a high standard (one was Dostoyevsky's *Crime and Punishment*, which I found other prisoners reading, too). He asked for a detailed account of our job, then gave us a lucid analysis of his own conditions of detention, observing they could not but be called inhuman or degrading for a host of reasons that he then listed in neat order. He pointed out that his contacts with the outside world were very limited, because he was allowed to see his family only once a week and had to speak to them through bullet-proof glass; besides, his conversations were recorded, for security reasons. Likewise, he was not allowed to see any friends and all his correspondence was censured. We made no comment, but his analysis of his conditions was accurate.

8

Policemen, Prison Warders and Magistrates

During our inspections our main point of reference within the state apparatus was not the high-ranking official at ministerial level. We did meet such officials to exchange formalities, often a tedious business, to the point that these grey men have already disappeared from my memory. Naturally, our real interlocutors were those representatives of the state who work 'in the field', in police stations, prisons and other penal institutions: policemen, prison warders and magistrates.

Our relations with them were not always easy. An inspector is bound to be a nuisance, for anyone; when the inspector is also a foreigner and does not speak your native tongue this can only lead to greater hostility and suspicion. Often, under a courteous and respectful guise, we could feel their irritation at what was seen to be an undue intrusion into a reserved area.

This attitude was particularly noticeable among the police, especially lower-ranking officers. The latter are used to dealing with people (both suspects and criminals) who often come from the lowest levels of society and have a poor cultural background; somehow the coarseness of behaviour and rudimentary psychology of those people is transmitted to the policemen who are used to dealing with them. Besides, these very officers come from cultural and educational backgrounds that sometimes do not differ very much from those of the individuals they have to apprehend and arrest. Hence their rough and aggressive manner with the underdogs, an attitude that frequently goes with servility to people in higher authority. Such was the attitude of many policemen towards us: oscillating between brusque, irritable manners and a measure of subservience. Added to this was the fact that, as I have already remarked, policemen used to interrogating others found it very unnatural, and even insulting, to be inspected by us: to be the object of searching questions, to be asked to explain their behaviour, to be requested firmly to produce objects and documents, to open certain cupboards, unlock certain doors, and show us anything we wanted to see.

It is hardly surprising, therefore, that we often felt we were playing cat and mouse with the police: we sensed they were trying to hide something, or to put us on the wrong track, and that we would have to play a cunning hand and think fast to forestall their next move. Sometimes, perhaps, we were able to do so. At other times, we failed: the disappointing results of our inspections (unsatisfactory compared with what we had been led to expect, after receiving credible information), together with the sly smiles I caught on the faces of a few policemen, confirmed our impression of having got nowhere.

Nor is it surprising that we sometimes provoked the rage of a policeman. Thus, I remember the furious words of an officer in a police station, who arrogantly demanded, at the top of his voice, why we were so eager to protect the rights of terrorists in jail, instead of worrying about the conditions of the numerous relatives of policemen killed by terrorists. We had to explain, with great calm, exactly what our job implied and what our mandate was, saying that unfortunately we could do nothing for these relatives, even though we shared his feelings of grief. Our job was to protect anyone deprived of his or her liberty from possible abuse at the hands of the government authorities, and this included terrorists and the worst sorts of criminal.

On another occasion, one of the chief inspectors of a large police station had followed us all over the building, of which he directed one section. He did so with increasing signs of impatience at our meticulous scrutiny of each room, the care with which we looked through the contents of each cupboard and perused the custody registers. When, after speaking to various inmates in private, some of my colleagues asked for a collective interview with a group of detainees in the large, dark and evil-smelling security cell where they were being held, something made him lose his temper. He started to yell furiously, shouting that we had gone too far: our aim was obviously to make anti-police propaganda, and we wanted to dishonour the state officials of that nation. I had to ask him to calm down and to respect our right of inspection. Since he continued to scream, and was about to block the entrance to the security cell to prevent my colleagues from getting on with their work, I had to ask him for his name and rank, adding that I would have to report his behaviour to the Ministry of the Interior the next day. Even this did not calm him down; but on noticing how the detainees (well used to his arrogance) were observing with delight his furious outbursts and his sense of humiliation, together with the arrival of a colleague who whispered a few words in his ear, he walked out, slamming the door behind him. We did not see him again, and preferred to forget the incident.

In another country, during the inspection of a huge police station, I had noticed that one of the officers, who was walking round with us, was quivering with indignation. He was middle-aged, short and red-faced. He looked as if he might have worked his way up from the bottom, getting promoted for sheer hard work. His face clearly revealed his anger. At one point, while my colleagues were talking to a group of suspects, I took him on one side and started to question him affably on the daily routine of the station, the stress to which policemen were subjected, the effects this had on their family life. After a little he let the cat out of the bag, almost with relief. He was one of several policemen in that town and elsewhere who felt deeply irritated and offended at our presence: our job as inspectors was to prevent torture, therefore by going to that country we obviously suspected cases of torture. He found the very idea that we could imagine the national police capable of torture humiliating and infuriating. Now that he had given vent to his anger, he wanted to know what I thought. I told him he was quite right, it was out of the question that the police in his country would use torture: we had been well aware of this when we began our visit; our impression had then been confirmed by our investigations. But he was wrong – I added – to think of our task as only covering torture. I then explained that we were also expected to prevent ill-treatment and abuse, and unfortunately there were quite a few cases of this in his country, as we had discovered for ourselves.

During our inspections we came across all sorts of policemen: some were courteous and intelligent; others brutish and rude. Two, in particular, stand out in my mind, perhaps because they were symbolic of the two extremes.

I met the first at the airport in the capital of a large country. We had been there for a week already and decided to visit the premises we knew to be at the airport, in which foreigners were held while their requests for asylum were being examined. We were greeted by a lively and pleasant-mannered chief inspector, who took us urbanely round the whole of the huge airport – more like a half-hidden metropolis, astonishing in its size, complex organization and stratified hierarchy. The inspector was short and very neatly dressed, with a friendly but reserved manner, as if to say: I've seen so much in my life that I'm hardly going to be impressed by you and all your questions. He seemed the personification of Maigret, relaxed in manner and with a drawl. He agreed to each one of our requests, driving us from one end of the airport to the other in his own car. He showed us everything we wanted to see and gave detailed answers to our questions. From time to time, excusing himself with a polite smile and mentioning the pressing calls of duty, he would leave us in the hands of one of his underlings (one of these, a fairly high-ranking inspector, was an engaging and elegant woman; you could have imagined her as a member of the upper bourgeoisie out on a shopping spree, had it not been for her hawk-like eyes and the large pistol I glimpsed in her handbag, which made all the metal detectors jump wherever we went).

The other man I met in the anti-terrorist section of a middle-sized police station, in another country. We had received sinister reports on that section, and so were very meticulous in our inspection. There were very few inmates, and they were all reticent. We checked the registers: the police station, which was usually bursting at the seams, had suddenly emptied, as if by magic, the previous day. One of the officers taking us round was about thirty, in plain clothes, a very lean body and great circles under his eyes, reddish hair and a forced smile. After a while, we realized he was one of the men who conducted interrogations in the anti-terrorist section. He was one of the quickest in giving us explanations and seemed very well informed on the relevant national legislation. For this reason I stopped to ask him about methods of interrogation and about his own experiences. On being alone with me and the interpreter, he looked embarrassed and reluctant to talk. His answers were evasive or routine, and he would glance sideways, every now and then, as if to check something. When we took our leave, disappointed at having found so little, I shook hands with him, too, and found to my surprise that his hand was sweaty, almost wet. Later I remarked on the fact to my colleague, adding that the man must have been rather nervous, judging by his damp handshake.

I remembered this incident three days later. I was in a prison, talking to people who had been held fairly recently in that police station, especially those who had been in the anti-terrorist section. After a long day of meetings, the interpreter and I entered a cell where there were two women. One was very young; we had been given her name by several other detainees who had caught sight of her in the anti-terrorist section. The other was an elderly, matronly woman, with an air of distinction. We began to talk to the latter, because she seemed ready to do so. She not only recounted how she had been treated in prison (on the whole, she had no complaints), but also how she had been arrested and then, little by little, the whole story of her life: how she had fallen low, from material comfort to poverty and squalor because of drugs, until she had committed the crime for which she had been arrested and convicted. After such a fluent account, made (so the interpreter told me) in cultivated language, we had not a little trouble in getting the girl who was sitting on the next bed in the same cell to speak. She was pale and thin and could not have been over twenty, though her drawn and sickly face made her look older. Little by little, thanks to the older woman's encouragement and the gentle manner of the interpreter, we got some information. She gave a jump when I began to ask specific questions about the police station and stopped talking. It took all the kindly insistence of the other woman to get her to speak again. So, a few words at a time, she described the techniques of her interrogation, the torture and ill-treatment to which she had been subjected. Though she was talking faster, there was a slight reticence in her voice. The other prisoner had noticed this and interrupted us to say that the young woman had been raped in that police station during her interrogation; we had to be told, even though the girl did not have the strength to mention it. We sat in silence, then I broke it by telling the girl I quite understood her feelings, she need not tell us about it: it was not our intention to increase her suffering by opening such fresh wounds. Then, having translated my words, in a very natural manner the interpreter gave tangible proof of this by stroking her face. At this the girl pulled herself together and said firmly no, she had to tell us, because it was right for people to know what she had been through; she would be glad if we told the government authorities and informed public opinion. I asked if she would rather speak to a woman colleague of mine. It did not make any difference, she said, my being a man: the important thing was that it should be known. Thus she told us how she had not only been tortured, but raped by one of the policemen – and gave us a thumbnail sketch of the events. At one stage I noticed that the interpreter was no longer translating my words, but was talking excitedly to her. I was surprised, because the interpreter – a middle-aged woman who was both competent and highly intuitive – had always behaved in a very professional manner, carrying out her duties with great care. I noticed she was feeling deeply shaken. A little later I discovered that the girl had given such an exact description of the rapist that, before my next question, the interpreter had started to ask questions of her own, to confirm her impression that this was the officer we had met a few days earlier. Having got the answers she wanted, she then translated them to me, adding with furious indignation that it had been that thin little man we had spoken to in the police station. The account had been so truthful and the fact that we had actually met the rapist had shaken the interpreter; she again forgot her detached and neutral attitude to her work, and asked me to do something, because what had happened to the girl was disgraceful. Then, at my request, she translated everything to the two prisoners, including my reply: unfortunately, we could do nothing, both because we could not give the authorities the source of our information, and because we had no right to demand an inquiry against the culprit. It was up to the girl to turn to the courts and accuse the policeman. My reaction provoked the elderly woman's rage and embarrassment. The girl merely shook her head, dejectedly, adding that no one would believe her, because she had no proof of having been tortured; it would have been a waste of time to denounce the rapist.

The next day we went back to the police station, to check certain points, but the thin little policeman was no longer there; I shall never know if he was not on duty that day, or if he had heard of our interview with the girl.

That evening, back in the hotel, I was reflecting on our impotence to do anything useful in single cases and recalled Camus' words in the *Mythe de Sisyphe*, which have haunted me for many years. In 1942 Camus wrote that there are only two 'answers', two 'ways of thinking' on all crucial issues, that is those issues which 'may lead to death or intensify the passion of living': the notary's bleak recording of reality (this was the method used by Monsieur de la Palisse); or an impassioned struggle, however naive and absurd (this was Don Quixote's reaction). That day, in that dingy prison, I had been forced simply to record the facts, as it were: this, and nothing more.

Prison officers are very different from policemen. Not many people wish to do their job: it is poorly paid, tiring and fairly squalid; it does not have the glamour that the man in the street attributes to policing. The policeman's job is to search for truth, to descend into the sinks of iniquity to capture criminals; a policeman risks his life to protect respectable people. His work is exalted in books, on the radio and television, and at the cinema. A policeman is astute and strong, he uses violence to a good end. By watching a detective on the television screen, we satisfy our own repressed instincts to do violence without suffering any guilt.

Prison warders have no literary charm, nor does their work satisfy our subterranean impulses. They usually come from a background of poverty and take the job only for want of a better one. They spend their days cheek by jowl with people who have been exiled far from human society and shut up in these 'social dustbins'. They are shipwrecked men supervising other castaways. Thus they become, unawares, vehicles for taming transgressors. Michel Foucault calls them 'professionals of discipline, normality and subjection'. Certainly, their main task is to 'normalize' the detainees.

Our experience as inspectors revealed that warders are far readier than the police to collaborate, to give an exact description of the reality in which they spend their days. To a certain extent this may depend on the fact that prisons are vast and complex structures. Responsibility for the organization of penitentiaries, for decisions taken and measures adopted, are watered down and spread out among numerous members of staff; often decisions are made by authorities who live far away, in the capital. Besides, to a certain extent, prison warders lead the same lives as detainees: they spend most of their time in jail; this makes them sensitive to the prevailing climate in that institution, and it is in their own interests to keep the level of tension low. This is particularly true of long-term prisons: here the warders know they will have to live side by side with the same prisoners for a long time, and they do their best to avoid friction. The best way to eschew conflict is to allow prisoners to lead lives that are as little inhuman as possible, offering such activities as work, sport, recreation and so on, and numerous opportunities for socializing. In a nutshell, their job is to distract the mind from the oppressiveness of life in prison.

Perhaps this explains why we found prison staff so genuinely interested in our assessment and criticism. Thus, at the end of an inspection, we would always meet the prison governor and senior members of staff to talk about what we had seen and to discuss our suggestions for improvements. In quite a few instances the governor fully agreed with our criticisms, often having reached the same conclusions some time earlier: consultation with the government authorities had been to no avail.

One group of judicial officials with whom we had only sporadic and superficial contact were the magistrates. In some countries we met several public prosecutors, or other inquiring magistrates, who would rush to the police stations under their authority as soon as they heard we had begun an inspection there. But this was only a formality: they merely wanted to inform us, by their physical presence, that the police depended on them, and that therefore they took full responsibility for what went on there. Yet after a few polite but pertinent questions, we were confirmed in our belief that these magistrates have only perfunctory control over how the police behave. In some countries the inquiring magistrates are vaguely aware that the police can commit abuse, but they prefer not to go into the matter; they often believe that rough and ready methods are the most effective with suspects. They are prepared to deal with abuse and ill-treatment only if they are formally required to do so, after the victim has made a specific charge. In other words, they wait for the person who has been cruelly treated or bullied to go through the solemn ritual of presenting a formal charge. By so doing they ignore – or pretend to ignore – the fact that most persons held in police custody are extremely vulnerable, as I have remarked in a previous chapter. I should add that I have even come across cases where the inquiring magistrate prefers to overlook cases when the victim has made a formal charge. In one country we visited, charges can only be made at the police stations; it follows that if the inquiring magistrate is told by a person that he has been ill-treated by the police while in custody, he normally answers that he is 'not competent' to receive such charges. In that country, an influential lawyer, himself the victim of torture and other atrocities at the hands of a by-gone dictatorship, told me the story of a recent episode. One day he was standing in the office of an inquiring magistrate on official business, when a detainee entered with his lawyer and two policemen; the young man came from a good family and had been caught for a serious case of theft; his arrest had to be confirmed. Before the magistrate could fill in the various forms, the young man's lawyer pointed out that his client had been repeatedly and savagely beaten by the police; so saying, he raised the boy's shirt and showed the bruises on his arms and chest. The magistrate countered at once that it was no concern of his: such claims were beyond his powers. At this point the lawyer who was telling me the story, remembering what it felt like to be tortured, felt obliged to intervene to tell the magistrate in no uncertain terms that his attitude was absurd; did he expect the young man to hand in his official complaint to the very police who had beaten him up? There was a sharp altercation between the two, then the magistrate reluctantly recorded the charge; later, thanks to this charge, the police were prosecuted in a trial that aroused considerable public interest.

The same can be said for judges supervising prisons. In various countries they have a great deal of power and should keep an eye on how prisoners are treated and how the penitentiary is administered. To judge from the interviews I had with many of them, those magistrates tend to maintain a very bureaucratic approach to inmates and jails: they check the files and, at most, they may pay scrupulous attention to a single case, talking to individual prisoners in the room set aside for this purpose; they may even work hard to obtain a reduction of specific prisoners' sentences, or get permission for them to see relatives, or merely give advice. However, they never, or hardly ever, set foot in the prisoners' cells. It is as if these judges preferred to leave the administration of a penitentiary entirely in the hands of the bureaucrats paid to do so – the governor and his staff – respecting an absurd and pernicious distribution of tasks among different government departments.

I met many of these magistrates and, unfortunately, I always found the experience disappointing. I got the impression that supervisory judges are often rather grey characters, who regard their job as a sort of covert punishment. They would far rather sit in court and deal with the mountainous paperwork of a trial; they would prefer to belong to what they believe to be the real world of legal process, rather than having to take an interest in sorry cases of unsavoury criminals. More than once, we got tangible proof of the limits to these judges' training, in various countries: many of them know their law backwards, but have no interest in or knowledge of social and psychological issues, particularly with regard to foreigners, a category greatly at risk in Europe.

In a nutshell, many judges seem to show little interest in what befalls single individuals. It is hardly surprising that one of the few magistrates to make an impression on my memory was rather a caricature. A few hours after beginning our visit to a large prison, this judge asked to see us in his office. Though irritated at the interruption, I felt it my duty to meet the man; I went to see him with a colleague, an interpreter and the prison governor. The man was middle-aged, very thin, exceedingly elegant, with a long face, a hooked nose and quicksilver eyes. He was falsely welcoming, with a bombastic manner perfectly mirrored in the pomp of his elegant office. We soon became aware of great friction between him and the governor, whom he wanted to humiliate in our presence to underscore the fact that he was the real authority in that penitentiary. To show off his superiority he immediately stated that he did not require the services of the interpreter; as the members of our delegation and the interpreter used English (i.e. we spoke 'fluently though in broken English', as Robinson Crusoe said of Man Friday), he started to speak to us in a very halting version of that language. What he had to say was so banal that we soon tried to take our leave. He insisted on coming too. Having discovered I was Italian, as we walked down long corridors and crossed dingy halls, he announced in triumph that he had been several times to Rome, had met some of his opposite numbers at the Ministry of Justice and had learnt to speak Italian. He then fell silent for a while as he racked his brain and we walked on down corridors that were ever darker and dirtier, with him trotting behind. After a little he spluttered out phrases such as 'cordiali saluti!' ('yours sincerely'), 'egregio collega' ('esteemed colleague'), 'mi creda suo devotissimo' ('I am, believe me, your most devoted servant'), 'eccellenza' ('Excellency'), each utterance followed by long thoughtful pauses. He delivered these phrases in a sonorous voice, rolling a triumphant eye at me and on the mortified governor, who followed wearily behind.

Apart from this preposterous magistrate, of the many judges I met, none left an impression, except for the one I mentioned in chapter 4, whom indeed, I find it impossible to forget. There was nothing remarkable about his appearance, he looked like a second-rate bureaucrat: short and plump, his sparse hair turning grey, a grizzled moustache, ordinary clothes, a large gold ring on his left hand and glasses with heavy frames, which hid a lively pair of eyes. The first time we went to see him was to ask for his authorization to visit the hidden area of a large police station; he greeted us with politeness and curiosity. I was surprised that on entering his fortress offices, apparently besieged by dozens of policemen and bodyguards all armed to the teeth, we were not frisked, nor made to pass through a metal detector, and were not even asked to display our IDs. The judge was well aware who we were, but he was known to be very suspicious, for good reason, since he had already been the target of terrorist attacks, and headed the list of intended victims. I concluded the absence of any check on us was a deliberate form of courtesy, and felt it augured well for our difficult mission.

After an exchange of official phrases and seeing that I was about to make my request, he stopped me with a polite but peremptory gesture, sat down behind his desk, and pressed a button on the tape recorder that sat on top of a pile of books and files. Then, having noticed my surprise, he explained that he did not say or listen to anything unless he recorded it on tape. All we said was then recorded: if the tape ended mid-sentence, he would raise his hand to ask for silence, change the tape calmly, set it in motion and ask us to carry on. He told us at once that he greatly appreciated our rule of secrecy, since it was one he too had to follow (this was probably one of the main reasons he was to be so open-handed with us, at least in some respects).

In our first meeting, arguing from opposite points of view, each firmly defending their own opinion, he observed us with a ceremonious, though wily, look, reminiscent of a cat watching a mouse it is about to catch. He was very clear in transmitting to us that he had the whiphand: he pointed out that in his country inquiring magistrates did not depend on the Executive, that he took

118

orders from no one, not even from the Prime Minister or Head of State. 'And,' he added with a rather complacent smile, 'I only receive those I wish to see; for instance, two days ago, despite the Premier's insistence, I refused to meet a high-ranking politician from an important foreign state' (and he told us who this was). Then he said, heatedly brandishing a well-thumbed volume he had on his desk, he would only take orders from that book (the Constitution, the penal code, and the code of criminal procedure). He added that he had full power over us: he could institute inquiries into our activities, even though he was now meeting us in person. Naturally, in my reply, I thanked him tangentially for the honour he did us in letting us meet him, though I said nothing of his claim to start inquiries on us, since our immunity and privileges were backed by international guarantee.

At the end of our exhausting first interview, we emerged victorious, as I described in chapter 4. As we shook hands, he remarked with a sly smile, that he thought we would meet again soon, and that perhaps we would 'become friends'. We left that fortress feeling euphoric, because we had the authorization we needed. But we also felt uneasy, because the man we had met was ambiguous: he was obviously highly intelligent, yet he had reached the pinnacle of a state apparatus which seriously ill-treated (of this we had abundant and concordant proof) people accused or suspected of serious crimes. Why had he been so friendly, since he was known to be arrogant and proud of his great power? Why had he allowed us into that prohibited area, after stating that he thought we had no right to go there?

We went back to see him a few days later. In fact, after that first interview, when we returned to the notorious police station, we had the distinct impression, as we inspected the various security cells, that one or more prisoners had been removed earlier. Knowing full well that nothing could happen in that police station without the magistrate's permission, I suggested we return to see him. Some of our group were very reluctant: he would have refused to see us, as he would have been informed of our very careful inspection, and could easily imagine what our conclusions were – devastating for the men under his command; I was also warned not to be enmeshed by the man's wiles, since he was known not only to be enormously powerful but to defend the behaviour of his policemen always. In a nutshell, for some of my colleagues he had become Evil incarnate and we must not fall into his trap.

After a sleepless night (due also to overtiredness) I decided to make a try. I disliked the idea that he might refuse to receive us. Thus we decided on an unorthodox way of asking for an interview. We went to his 'fortress' and, from the guard-room, we phoned through to his secretary to say we were passing by and had not forgotten his phrase about meeting again and 'becoming friends': we would be delighted to spend no more than ten minutes with him, if that were possible. To my surprise, we were ushered in at once (as we entered his office, two very haughty gentlemen left hurriedly and in a huff). We then spent two and a half hours with him. I came straight to the point: did he know some detainees had been taken away from the police station while we were inspecting it? He replied that not only did he know about their removal, but it had been done at his express order. Dismayed, I asked why he had done so: he said he was determined those prisoners should not speak to us, so long as the inquiry was being held. I countered this statement with my own legal arguments. He listened placidly, with a smile of satisfaction: then he advanced his own deductions. After a tiring exchange, I suggested we follow the practice often adopted in the United Nations of agreeing to disagree. He nodded his consent; he knew he had won that battle.

But he wished to show us his magnanimity by promising to let us speak to the detainees before we left the country; we could count on it, he added with an air of omnipotence. Then he talked of his life in that bunker, surrounded by bodyguards, his excessive weight due to a sedentary life (he was offering us some sweetmeats and apologized for not taking any himself, but he had to keep his weight down). Then he showed us two films of terrorists being questioned on the large television screen in his office. As we watched, he remarked that, as we could see, these persons were talking freely of their crimes and showed no signs of ill-treatment, nor were they being bullied during their confessions. It served no purpose to tell him what we found obvious: those were not films of interrogations, but 'spontaneous confessions', probably made just after the real interrogation. This was apparent from the lack of expression, the monotonous voice, the apparent lack of any emotion with which these detainees told the story of the horrible crimes they had committed. Looking straight at the video camera, they seemed to be reciting, unwillingly, a long flat monologue which they had been forced to learn by heart: there was no break in the voice, no tremor of the facial muscles; they looked like talking statues, like the living dead. The judge appeared not to notice the discrepancy and observed us with a satisfied smile.

We left, feeling depressed and downcast. Did he really think he had outwitted us? Or was he himself being tricked by the fog of his own political fanaticism and legal delusions? We decided not to see him again. Yet we did meet again, twice. This was two years later, in his office, where he sat, looking a little greyer and very tired. I was struck by the fact that he did not mention our reports, which had been very harsh, though they lay on his table. I shall never know if his mind was obfuscated by a deformed sense of legality and an aberrant faith in the idea that the state should be defended at all costs and by any means, however pitiless and violent, against any attempt to sub-vert or destroy it. Or whether he had a clear picture of the appalling abuse and arbitrary behaviour of his men, con-doning it for reasons of state. He asked us if we could name the police officers we held to be guilty of ill-treating detainees: he would immediately prosecute them. We said it was not our job to give him these names, all the more so as we never asked the police for their names and rank; it was his job to initiate criminal proceedings, if he believed what lay written in our reports. On that occasion I felt his question was merely a subtle way of defending his state, with false and hypocritical offers of action, which were intended as a smoke-screen to hide the real facts.

9

A Few Concluding Observations

In 1989, when I was elected a member and then president of the Committee, several friends asked me if I had taken on such an onerous task because it was a highly paid job. When I answered that I would get no remuneration, they shook their heads in puzzlement. I, too, have asked myself more than once why I had taken on such a Herculean labour. Perhaps I needed 'to work the fat off my soul'; after spending so many years deciphering reality through books and at diplomatic conferences, I felt the need to stretch out my hands and touch that reality. And like many naive and inexperienced persons, I discovered I had plunged in at the deepest and roughest end. Together with these possible, subjective motives – of little or no interest to the reader – there was also my long-standing interest in human rights and a strong desire to give substance to that interest. In less abstract terms, I longed to lend a hand in fleshing out those rights. To borrow Kafka's graphic metaphor: mine was a desire not merely to throw open the window and stand looking down into the night, after hearing cries coming from 'a small stone quarry, deserted and bleak' where someone was being murdered, but to rush down and help that victim chase off the aggressor.

After almost four years' work it is difficult to take stock.

Having read those of the Committee's reports that have been made public, an acquaintance teasingly suggested I should write a 'guide to all the most horrible places in Europe': a Baedeker to what no one should ever visit. Indeed, the material is not lacking. But this is not the point. From a personal point of view, these years of arduous effort have not been altogether gratifying. Naturally, it was very satisfying to have helped to institute and set in motion a well-functioning and important international mechanism. It was gratifying to throw one's passionate energy into creating a legal mechanism for which almost everything had to be invented and, thereby, to have disproved Hegel's arid and dour comment that 'It is a poor substitute to make into the source of right our natural or our worked up feelings and the inspirations of our own hearts.' Yet on another plane – that of descending into the quarry to help a possible victim escape the aggressor – my hopes have been disappointed. Far too often my colleagues and I have had to act as the notaries of other people's suffering. But for exceptional cases (such as when inspectors make the immediate observations I mentioned in chapter 4, followed by the closure or demolition of intolerable detention areas or the transfer of inmates from cramped and unhygienic cells), our work bears fruit mainly in the long term. We are able to make changes for the future, but cannot introduce immediate improvements for specific individuals. It is certainly a comfort to see a disheartened and glum detainee smile after a long interview; but this hardly corresponds to the hopes Beccaria expressed with amazing innocence ('If, by championing the rights of men and of invincible truth, I shall contribute to save from agony and anguish one unfortunate victim of tyranny or of ignorance [. . .] the blessings and tears of transport of one innocent will be sufficient consolation to me for the contempt of all mankind').

124

All too often, after visiting a particularly oppressive penitentiary, where we had met with suffering and humiliation without being able to do anything that would bring immediate relief, I felt like one standing in the chorus in an early Greek tragedy. I too could identify with the tribulations of the main characters, trying to understand the causes, brooding on the human condition, but aware of man's powerlessness to change the course of events. Let me, however, leave aside such subjective considerations and turn to three reflections of a general nature.

First, our investigations allowed us to conclude that conditions of detention are still very backward in most European states. I realize that several governments have accused the Strasbourg inspectors of choosing to visit institutions that are most at risk, of having highlighted shadowy areas and neglected those in full sunlight. Yet our choice was sound. Let us not forget that any medium-sized European state has hundreds of police stations, dozens of jails, numerous hospitals where people are held against their will, or detention centres for foreigners, not to mention many other institutions where the authorities detain people by force. How could we ever visit them all? We had to make a selection, placing institutions where inhuman treatment is most likely at the top of our list. Furthermore, on more than one occasion we inspected prisons or police stations that were impeccable, and we always mentioned these in our final reports. Even so, with a heavy heart I am forced to conclude that no European country is blameless. Many have overcrowded jails, with inadequate sanitation, or insufficient regime activities (work opportunities, vocational training and recreational facilities). In other cases solitary confinement is applied far too frequently. Let me quote the words of a public prosecutor in Rome – a woman whose rigour and humanity one cannot but admire – that sum up the situation, and not for Italy only: 'What is a prison? It is a

125

place where one loses not only one's liberty, but one's dignity, too. Whenever I send someone to jail, I suffer, too.' In other states it is the police stations that invite criticism: in some countries the physical conditions in detention cells are intolerable (cramped, dark, dirty and airless); in a few the police ill-treat or even torture the inmates. In other states the detention centres for immigrants or for asylum seekers are unhygienic and inhuman. In yet other countries the psychiatric institutions and hospitals to which detainees are sent are seriously substandard. When several of these deficiencies are combined, the overall picture is an alarming one. Of course, there are considerable differences between one country and the next. In some (only three perhaps) torture is embedded in police methods; in others the police tend sporadically to ill-treat and brutalize their detainees; in other states the prisons reveal aspects censurable as inhuman or degrading; elsewhere single instances of arbitrary behaviour by law enforcement officers can be discerned, or there are single cases of unacceptable treatment or conditions in prisons or hospitals. Despite the many different degrees of substandard treatment, not one European state fully conforms to the parameters of the best and most enlightened traditions and the more recent studies in criminology. Hence, the work of the inspectors is sacrosanct. Not only must they continue to carry out their helpful work of investigation and fact-finding, but they should continue to set up, as quickly as possible, a corpus of rules and standards that will complete and improve the European Prison Rules (which the Council of Europe's Committee of Ministers adopted in 1987, as a recommendation for member states; these, however, refer only to prisons and, besides, need now to be revised and updated). Obviously, such a corpus of rules and standards could have a notable impact on the daily activities of places of detention throughout Europe: it would be particularly useful in introducing, throughout the continent, the uniform application of highly ethical, as well as practical, laws and principles governing relations between state authorities and individuals deprived of their freedom.

My second reflection requires me to stand back and take the history of sociology as my point of departure. To a large extent the work of the Strasbourg inspectors has confirmed, though it has also partially belied, those 'two laws of penal evolution' laid down in 1901 by Emile Durkheim (in the *Année sociologique*). For the French sociologist the first law provides that 'the intensity of the punishment is proportional to the backwardness of a society and the authoritarian nature of the central government'. To clarify the meaning of this law, Durkheim drew a distinction between two types of criminality. First, there are crimes against collective values or assets such as religion, custom, traditions, the authority of the state and its representatives. These are 'religious crimes', because attacks on religion are the most conspicuous class of such offences; besides, even illegal acts against heads of state and other members of the Establishment assume the character of religious crimes: they too are forms of sacrilege. It is this sacrilegious nature that makes religious crimes both odious and intolerable, and their punishment so inexorable and violent. Indeed, the more a taboo is worthy of respect the more to break it is considered abominable. Furthermore, there is a huge difference between the magnitude of the deity (or the authority representing the deity) and the insignificance of the transgressor. Is any punishment sufficiently terrible for an individual who has offended against a god? Such crimes undermine the supreme values of the community: they are not prejudicial to the interests of an individual, they disrupt the religious, moral and ideological tenets on which society is founded. They are profoundly subversive

127

crimes. Thus, it is considered justifiable to inflict unprecedented cruelty and suffering on the reprobate.

The other kind of criminality includes crimes against individuals as such, that is persons divested of any transcendental or supra-individual attribute: theft, murder, violence and fraud of every kind. Such is the nature of what Durkheim terms 'human criminality'. When this kind of crime has to be punished, there is no longer that huge difference between the transgressor and the commandment which has been broken, typical of 'religious criminality'. Here, too, the crime provokes moral outrage, but it is less horrific, and therefore requires a less exemplary and violent response. According to Durkheim, with the advance of civilization, religious criminality is replaced by its human form: by the same token, a very heavy-handed and exemplary penal repression gives way to milder and, as it were, more humane forms. (However, one exception is modern despotism, where the repressive regime needs to defend itself by raising any crime against its authority to a form of religious criminality, with obvious consequences for the level of repression.)

Durkheim's second law lays down that 'sentences aimed at depriving individuals of their freedom, for varying lengths of time according to the gravity of the crime, tend more and more to become the normal form of penal repression'. As we know, prison is an essentially modern institution. Although it existed in antiquity, it was used mainly to prevent the accused from running away or for persuading debtors to pay up, or even as a form of supplementary penalty. Most punishments were corporal: public flogging, mutilation, branding with a hot iron, the pillory, putting reprobates to death amid unspeakable torments (crucifixion, quartering, burning at the stake and other forms of torture). Exile was envisaged only in a few more progressive societies, and for quite specific crimes. By the end of the eighteenth century, thanks to a whole set of historical, social and economic reasons, governments start to use imprisonment – even though, up to the early twentieth century, supplementary punishment such as being chained, being deprived of food, and forced labour were added to the loss of freedom. Indeed, as the second category of crime ('human criminality') became more widespread and penal repression became correspondingly less violent, cruel and dramatic, the jail took over increasingly from the more archaic systems of punishment. Besides, supplementary forms of punishment gradually disappeared, until to be deprived of one's liberty prevailed as the most important and widespread form of expiation (though, of course, capital punishment still exists in many states). Furthermore, a prison is no longer conceived as a place of punishment, but as a place of healing, an institution in which the convict can, and must, be rehabilitated and learn to readapt to civilian society. All modern constitutions proclaim this principle.

Our inspections, indeed, confirmed the validity of these two laws, though they also revealed certain present-day phenomena which, in more than one case, may defeat them. We all know that this is an age in which crime is increasing at a stupefying rate. As I mentioned in chapter 1, we also know the reasons: the capillary spread of drugs and the existence of criminal groups, organized on a global scale, buying and selling narcotics; terrorism; unemployment and the ensuing social and economic unrest, which far from diminishing, is on the increase; immigration and all the consequent social conflict; and violence broadcast by the mass media, which becomes infectious. To these one should add another surprising phenomenon: many crimes (especially murder, kidnapping, rape and robbery) are increasingly savage. The ordinary citizen feels more and more insecure. The reaction of public opinion is to demand the exemplary punishment of criminals: once they have been arrested, they must get their deserts. Thus, the average person feels no indignation if the police handle suspects roughly during interrogation. If convicted, then people want such individuals to suffer in prison. It is thus considered acceptable for a jail to become an unbearable place in which convicts must purge themselves of the horrific acts committed while free. People want conditions to regress to those described by Beccaria, when he wrote that 'imprisonment is more a torment than a means of securing the person of the accused'. In other words, criminality is no longer 'religious', crimes are no longer acts of sacrilege or terrible transgressions against eternal and transcendental values; yet the public wishes the convict to be subjected to the same pitiless cruelty as that reserved for sacrilegious criminals in the past. Criminality has become 'human', but the repression of crime has gone back to the forms used against 'religious criminality'. In a preposterous application of the law of retaliation, the public demands that evil be punished evilly.

The consequences of this state of affairs is twofold for the Strasbourg inspectors. First, they have to go against the tide, knowing that they are setting themselves up against certain sectors of law enforcement agencies and of the bureaucracy of state repression, but also against the majority of public opinion. Second, for this very reason the inspectors' task is of crucial importance. If we wish to avoid that the conditions in detention centres be subjected once more to archaic values and forms of behaviour, then the inspectors must continue their visits with the same regularity and incisiveness. In the beginning we thought the Committee's work would soon be over. I remember a conversation with an official who acted as the Committee's liaison officer with the French government – he was the prefect who had become famous in Paris, in May 1968, when he had succeeded in preventing the political protest marches from degenerating into chaos: a lean and wiry man with hawk-like eyes. When I explained what we meant by the Committee's preventive function, he remarked: 'I've got it: you are working hard to be made redundant soon.' Alas, our experiences over the past years have proved that the Committee will not become superfluous either soon, or in the long run.

My third and last reflection is to wonder about the essence of the experience we accumulated over several years' inspection. How can we weigh up the initial reactions of the states concerned (whether favourable to the visits and receptive to our ensuing recommendations, or irritated by what was seen as an excessive interference by the Strasbourg Committee)? The inspectors' work and their pressing requests, presented to states in their reports, have proved one important point: by exercising, with courage and efficiency, those powers conferred on them by the Convention, they have breached a large gap – in real terms and not only on a legal plane – in the dogma of state sovereignty. This has happened at two distinct levels.

First, these international inspectors have been given free access – a few years back this would have been inconceivable – into the inner sanctum of the state: its police stations, jails, psychiatric institutions, military prisons, detention centres for aliens. In a way, they interposed themselves between people in custody, detainees, prisoners, convicts on the one hand and, on the other, the state bureaucrats (policemen, warders, judges) exercising powers of coercion over them. Thus, the inspectors penetrated – in actual fact and on every visit – into the most delicate and hidden recesses of the state machinery, scrutinizing and censuring its anomalies, defects and malformations.

At a later date the Strasbourg Committee intrudes in the internal affairs of states in a second way: after the inspection, there is a subsequent moment when the inspectors advance their criticisms, make suggestions, or request information. As soon as the inspectors urge states to modify or improve the state machinery, they inevitably advance deeply into the holy of holies of a sovereign state. For instance, when the Committee insists on respect for the four fundamental guarantees, which anyone taken into custody should enjoy (the right to legal counsel, the right to be examined by a doctor, the right to have one's family informed of one's arrest, the right to be informed of one's fundamental rights), in fact it is invading the state's legislative, judicial and administrative spheres. This became quite clear when we asked those governments that do not allow a lawyer immediate access to a person held in custody to guarantee this fundamental right. The reaction was a prompt reference to the obligations imposed by their own legislation. The inspectors did not lose heart, but insisted on these guarantees, suggesting that the government concerned should modify its laws.

The Committee was equally invasive when it exhorted a state to shorten the maximum period for police custody, so as to reduce opportunities for abuse at the hands of law enforcement officers. The same can be said of those occasions when the Committee severely censured the use of unhealthy and cramped detention cells, inviting the state in question to knock them down or to make radical changes: in such instances, the Strasbourg inspectors were actually asking that state to adopt administrative measures and, as a result, to shoulder what was often a hefty financial burden. This is also true of the recommendations the inspectors have made to several governments asking them to improve the training and education of their law enforcement officers, to introduce codes of behaviour, or to adopt specific rules on how to conduct the interrogation of people held in custody. An analogous form of interference was when the Committee asked states to put an end to overcrowding in prisons, pointing out that if this were aggravated by inadequate sanitation and the lack of regime activities, such overcrowding amounted to inhuman and degrading treatment. Equally intrusive has been the request to raise the standard of the medical service in jails (for instance, by making it part of the national health service, or at least by offering a service that is not inferior in quality to the latter).

If a state is to comply with so many demands it will have to introduce considerable reforms, at several levels: administrative, financial and social. In a nutshell, to carry out its preventive duties, the Committee has been forced to intrude not only into the daily administration of a state, but also into its legislative policy, into its plans for 'social engineering', as well as affecting certain decisions on the distribution of national resources. The Committee's interference may go further, suggesting choices to be made in a country's penal policy. Since its mandate is to prevent inhuman or degrading treatment, or to eliminate it wherever it exists, the Committee cannot but ask states – albeit indirectly, at times implicitly, with specific requests on specific issues – to practise a penal policy that is substantially based on resocializing and rehabilitating convicts. Such insistence is itself a form of interference in the country's legislative or administrative policy on the treatment of detainees.

It would be fatuous to object that, in all areas of governmental activity, states are used to receiving the recommendations of international organizations and that these are usually stillborn, for the very reason that they are no more than exhortations and promptings: acts that are never legally binding. This is true of such recommendations as are made by the United Nations and other intergovernmental organizations. Indeed, they are often drafted by diplomats, in very general terms; often the result of political and legal compromise, they almost always have to take account of the expectations and pressures of public opinion; besides, these acts are seldom accompanied by any system for checking their application. The Strasbourg Committee's recommendations are of a very different ilk. They are drafted and written by experts, with no political or diplomatic slant; they are specific, precise and exact, in other words they are 'targeted'. There is no intention of arousing public opinion, since they are destined to remain confidential (though the recipient government may, later, decide to put them in the public domain). Above all, these recommendations can never be mere hot air: the governments to whom they are addressed must decide on their implementation within precise time limits: three months, six months or one year. After receiving that government's reactions, the Committee evaluates them as more or less satisfactory; if they are considered unsatisfactory, then it can reiterate its prompting, and also decide to carry out another inspection in that country. Should the state continue to turn a deaf ear, the Committee can make the 'public statement' I mentioned in chapters 2 and 3: this is an important weapon by which to call the attention of world opinion and of other states in the Council of Europe to the deviant behaviour, and failure to cooperate, of recalcitrant governments.

Yet the strength of the Committee's recommendations lies mainly in that continuing dialogue between Strasbourg and each of the capitals in the twenty-three contracting states, which is set in motion after its first visit to a country. This dialogue represents a constant – and I might add, relentless – form of international pressure on each government to improve the situation in its territory. How effective it has proved to be is revealed by numerous circumstances. Let me mention again an episode I described in chapter 4. After a first visit to one of the twenty-three countries, the Committee had asked that the detention cells be radically modified or demolished in an important police station in that state. When the inspectors went back the second time they found that a new police station was being built, but this did not correspond to the requirements specified after the first visit; the government was urged to stop work on the site, pull down what had been built and construct the detention cells according to the inspectors' recommendations; on the third visit it was seen that the government had followed this advice and the relevant part of the building had been completely reconstructed. I feel the case is symbolic not only of the Committee's preventive mandate (what more effective way of preventing inhuman and degrading treatment than to make a pressing request to build completely new, roomy, healthy cells, with suitable sanitation?), but also of the Committee's intrusion into the domestic sphere of a state, not to mention the practical effects that mandate can have at a national level.

The Strasbourg Committee's authority to carry out this 'humanitarian interference' derives from the Convention by which it was instituted. It is, therefore, perfectly legitimate. Nevertheless, this approach is such an innovation that some states have proved dubious and recalcitrant. This is hardly surprising, as it is difficult to relinquish senescent mental patterns, superannuated forms of nationalism and the habitual refusal to allow supranational scrutiny. Little by little, I am sure, the more reluctant governments will get used to the intrusive visits of the Strasbourg inspectors, as well as to their pressing requests, their exhortations and their strictures.

Indeed, the experience of these first few years has shown that, despite the protests, friction and criticism, the work of the inspectors may occasionally provoke, it cannot but be beneficial. We must realize that – as I said in the Preface – a united Europe does not only mean having customs offices, banks, law firms and shops in common. It means introducing throughout Europe the values and standards of civilized behaviour that correspond to the best cultural traditions of our past. Let us not forget what Winston Churchill said in the House of Commons in 1910: one of the most unfailing tests of the civilization of any country is to see how the public and the authorities treat detainees. Therefore, if we really want a united, civilized and democratic Europe, we must prevent people detained for crimes of violence and abuse from being the object of cruel and humiliating treatment, perhaps less heinous than the crime for which they have been convicted, but equally unjustified.

To conclude: Theodor Mommsen, that enlightened liberal historian and great adversary of Bismarck's, nevertheless shared the latter's scorn for international treaties. Indeed, he described the 1899 Hague Conventions (the first major attempt to set limits to the violence of warfare) as 'a misprint in the history of mankind'. History has proved Mommsen wrong. Without that 'misprint', the barbarities of war would have been even greater (and in any case the importance of 'humanitarian rules' is to be seen not only in their ability to curtail our most aggressive impulses, but also in their enabling us to condemn those who transgress). Whatever one may think of the humanitarian law of armed conflict – which is being disregarded with such savagery, even now, in Europe: in the former Yugoslavia – there is no doubt that the European Convention for the Prevention of Torture can hardly be described as 'a misprint in the history of mankind'. On the contrary, it is a turning-point in the international struggle against the inhuman behaviour of man against man. Let us hope that, on the strength of that Convention, the inspectors will gradually extend their activities to other countries, even beyond the confines of Europe. Above all let us hope that, thanks to their daily efforts, humanity as a value will become the heritage of an increasing number of nations – albeit a heritage that we must continuously strive to preserve with all the patience and determination we can muster.

Note

In these additional pages I would like to give a few details on the setting up and operation of the group of inspectors.

The text by which the group was set up is an international treaty: the European Convention for the Prevention of Torture and Inhuman or Degrading Treatment or Punishment. The Convention was drafted within the Council of Europe, an intergovernmental organization with a membership of twenty-three states at the time and currently made up of thirty-eight states. At present member states include the fifteen countries of the European Union and other Western states such as Switzerland, as well as Mediterranean states such as Cyprus, Malta and Turkey and some former socialist countries – Albania, Bulgaria, the Czech Republic, Estonia, Hungary, Latvia, Lithuania Moldova, Poland, Romania, Russia, Slovakia, Slovenia and the Ukraine.

The Convention was drafted by two committees in the Council of Europe, both made up of 'government experts', that is experts appointed by the governments of the various member states, who in formal terms act in a personal capacity, though in reality they may act on government instructions. These two bodies are: the Steering Committee on Human Rights and the Committee of Experts for Developing the Rights laid down in the European Convention of Human Rights; the latter is an offshoot of the former (the author presided over the first of the two, having been vice-president of the second at an earlier date).

The Convention was opened for signature on 26 November 1987; it was ratified, over the next couple of years, by twenty-three countries: Austria, Belgium, Cyprus, Denmark, Finland, France, Germany, Great Britain, Greece, Iceland, Ireland, Italy, Liechtenstein, Luxembourg, Malta, the Netherlands, Norway, Portugal, San Marino, Spain, Sweden, Switzerland and Turkey. Gradually it was ratified by further states such as Bulgaria, the Czech Republic, Hungary, Poland, Romania, Slovakia and Slovenia. At present thirty states are bound by the Convention. Various countries that do not belong to the Council of Europe but are members of the OSCE (Organization for Security and Cooperation in Europe) have asked to become parties to the Convention (so far this can be ratified only by members of the Council of Europe). This has led to the adopting of an amending Protocol (no. 1) that will allow these states to join the Convention without belonging to the Strasbourg Organization. Other states, too, including some members of the Community of Independent States (CIS), have suggested they would like to receive the fact-finding visits of the Strasbourg inspectors, after signing *ad hoc* agreements and without being formally bound by the Convention. This should lead to the enlargement of the geographical area covered by the inspectors.

The Convention is a succinct text, which does not include substantial rules on torture or inhuman or degrading treatment: it merely sets up the European Committee for the Prevention of Torture and Inhuman or Degrading Treatment or Punishment, a body with the same number of members as the number of contracting parties. The members of the Committee are elected by the Council of Europe's highest political organ: the Committee of Ministers (made up of the Ministers of Foreign Affairs or Justice, or by ambassadors delegated by those ministers). The Committee of Ministers can elect only one of the three persons designated by the Consultative Assembly of the Council of Europe (made up of MPs from the various member states) and short-listed by the parliamentary delegation of each state (for example, the British parliamentary delegation draws up a list of three persons, who are then formally designated by the Consultative Assembly; the Committee of Ministers then elects one of the three). This was a way of guaranteeing a certain balance between parliamentary and executive bodies.

The inspectors have to be 'persons of high moral standing, well known for their knowledge in the field of human rights and for their professional experience in the spheres covered by the Convention' (Art. 4 of the Convention). Their mandate lasts four years, and could initially be renewed only once (though an amending Protocol, no. 2, was later adopted to allow for a member being re-elected twice).

The Committee, which began to operate in November 1989, has sent its delegations to all contracting states on periodic visits (to ensure impartiality, the order in which these visits were carried out has been decided, thus far, by drawing lots). There have also been nine *ad hoc* visits: two to Turkey and one each to Northern Ireland, Spain, Dutch Antilles and Aruba, Martinique, France, Sweden and Romania.

The inspectors' work is confidential (this is particularly true of the Committee's debates and decisions, the visit reports drawn up by the inspectors and the debate and voting on these reports). The only acts of the Committee that are public, besides the instituting Convention, are: the Rules of Procedure and the Annual Reports to the

Committee of Ministers and the Consultative Assembly of the Council of Europe. The Committee issued, on 15 December 1992, a Public Statement on Turkey (the sanction foreseen in Art. 10 (2) of the Convention for states that do not cooperate with the Committee or refuse to follow its recommendations). Although the inspectors' reports are always confidential, most countries have decided, with the Committee's approval, to make them public.

All public documents of the Committee can be obtained in one of the two official languages (English and French), from the Secretariat of the European Committee for the Prevention of Torture, (fax +33-88412772; tel. +33-88412000) or from the Council of Europe Press Department, Strasbourg (Ms S. Zimmer (fax +33-88412772; tel. +33-88412597))

For further reading on the Convention see: D. Vigny, 'La Convention européenne pour la prévention de la torture et des peines ou traitements inhumains ou dégradants', *Annuaire suisse de droit international*, 1987, pp. 43 ff.; E. Decaux, 'La Convention européenne pour la prévention de la torture et des peines et traitements inhumains ou dégradants', *Annuaire français de droit international*, 1988, pp. 618 ff.; A. Cassese, 'A New Approach to Human Rights: the European Convention for the Prevention of Torture', *American Journal of International Law*, 1989, pp. 128 ff. (also in French in *Revue génerale de droit international public*, 1989, pp. 5 ff.).

On the activities of the Committee, see M. Evans and R. Morgan, 'The European Convention for the Prevention of Torture: Operational Practice', *International and Comparative Law Quarterly*, 1992, pp. 590 ff., as well as my own brief remarks in *Rivista internazionale dei diritti dell'uomo*, 1992, pp. 11–14 and, at greater length, my essay 'The European Committee for the Prevention of Inhuman or Degrading Treatment or Punishment Comes of Age', in *Liber Amicorum H. G. Schermers*, 1994.

See also D. Fidler, 'The European Convention for the Prevention of Torture and Inhuman or Degrading Treatment or Punishment, opened for signature Nov. 26, 1987', *Harvard International Law Journal*, 1989, vol. 30, pp. 524–35; K. Ginther, 'The European Convention for the Prevention of Torture and Inhuman of Degrading Treatment or Punishment', *European Journal of International Law*, 1991, vol. 2 (no. 1), pp. 123–30; R. St. J. Macdonald, 'The European Convention for the Prevention of Torture and Inhuman or Degrading Treatment or Punishment', Chapter 22 in Essays in Honour of Judge Taslim Olawale Elias, (Bello and Ajibola eds.), vol. 1, 1992, pp. 399–426; S. Parmentier, 'Spotlight on Turkey: a Public Statement by the Committee for the Prevention of Torture', *Netherlands Quarterly for Human Rights*, 1993, pp. 131–6; G. Cohen-Jonathan, 'Le Comité européen pour la prevention de la torture et la declaration publique relative à la Turquie', *Revue générale de droit international public*, 1993, pp. 419–28; A. Tanca, 'The Public Statement on Turkey by the European Committee for the Prevention of Torture', *European Journal of International Law*, 1993, pp. 115–18; M. Evans and R. Morgan, 'The European Torture Committee: Membership Issues', *European Journal of International Law*, 1994, vol. 5 (no. 2), pp. 249–58; J. Murdoch, 'The Work of the Council of Europe's Torture Committee', *European Journal of International Law*, 1994, vol. 5 (no. 2), pp. 220–48; A. Salado Osuna, 'Las functiones del Comité europeo para la prevención de la tortura', *Revista de Instituciones Europeas*, 1994, vol. 21, pp. 563–81.